The Orchid in Lore and Legend

The Orchid in Lore and Legend

Luigi Berliocchi

translated by Lenore Rosenberg and
Anita Weston

edited by Mark Griffiths

TIMBER PRESS
Portland, Oregon

Printed in Hong Kong

Timber Press, Inc.
The Haseltine Building
133 S.W. Second Avenue, Suite 450
Portland, Oregon 97204, U.S.A.

Library of Congress Cataloging-in-Publication Data

Berliocchi, Luigi, 1953–
    [Fiore degli dei, l'orchidea dal mito alla storia. English]
    The orchid in lore and legend / Luigi Berliocchi ; translated by Lenore Rosenberg
and Anita Weston. ; edited by Mark Griffiths.
        p. cm.
    Includes bibliographical references (p.).
    ISBN 0-88192-491-1
    1. Orchids—History. 2. Orchids—Varieties. 3. Orchid culture. I. Griffiths, Mark,
1963– II. Title.

SB409.48 .B4713 2000
635.9'344—dc21

                                                                00-056829

Contents

Color plates follow page 160

Foreword

IT IS WONDERFUL to be able to welcome this translation of Luigi Berliocchi's exquisite masterpiece, *Il Fiore Degli Dei*. The pure poetry of his Italian prose has been beautifully translated under the editorship of Mark Griffiths into English that never betrays its Continental roots. Signor Berliocchi is a true collector—a bibliophile, polymath, and wordsmith who in this book has combined for our delight the magic, the history and botany, the folklore and medicinal values with the culture of those most mysterious of plants: orchids. He has produced a treasure-house of the legends that surround them that stands comparison with Sir James Frazer's *The Golden Bough*, taking us from Chinese antiquity to the plant collectors of the past three centuries. He tells us how the orchids gained their names and where and how they grow; he links the explorers to their plants, highlighting those who launched the orchidmania of the nineteenth century and leaving no fascinating nugget unexplored, be it the mimicry of *Ophrys*, the pollination of *Paphiopedilum*, the role of orchids in literature from Confucius to Proust via Oscar Wilde and H. G. Wells, the appearance of orchids in fossil strata, even the variety of composts.

I have read this book from the Contents to the Index without pause—all plant enthusiasts (not just orchidophiles) should do the same and then read it again. It is a reference book not just for its cornucopia of information but for the wealth of engravings and paintings that adorn almost every page. There has been no better book than this on the extraordinary story of the orchid, the flower of the gods, and it will be the standard by which all others are judged in the future.

DR. HENRY OAKELEY
Chairman, Royal Horticultural Society Orchid Committee

Preface

Exotic orchids have been part of our lives for more than two hundred years. Books and theses without number have been written to delineate their structures and unravel the mysteries of their physiology but all this knowledge has not diminished by one iota the intense fascination that is aroused in all of us, who having once seen them fall under their spell. They have a magic whose secret will always elude us, a blend of witchcraft and romance, that sets them apart, above all other plants—a sorcery that conjures up our deepest passions, from idolatrous worship through the pure spirituality of aesthetic veneration to fear, revulsion, and mindless hatred.

Even the name, orchid, hides the threat of sexual potency and desire behind the façade of its Greek roots, augmented by the origin of orchids on trees from distant lands, with no more nourishment than the air and water that melds with the rough bark on which they grow. From the myriad of shapes that cloak these plants come flowers of such forms and colors, evoking a fantasy of psychedelic imagery—from animistic theology to the most exquisite mimicry. Magnificent and perfect—designed, decorated, and embellished by invisible hands—and then, by the most divine irony, orchids have been hidden from humankind for millennia in the highest branches of the great trees of these long inaccessible tropical forests.

Our knowledge of orchids begins with the botanical texts of the second half of the eighteenth century when impassioned explorers on voyages of discovery in tiny sailing ships, or in far-flung corners of long-departed empires, collected, collated, and cataloged, and pressed, painted, and analyzed the floral riches of these distant worlds, driven by the forces of scientific inquiry that so dominated the age. Brought back to Europe, they were greeted with wonder, initially in the great botanic gardens such as those at Kew and Hamburg, but rapidly taken up by the great and wealthy who vied in the building of glasshouses to shelter their burgeoning and increasingly fabulous collections. These were the only people who could afford the vast expense of orchid growing, measured in the lives of the collectors who risked all in collecting from the remotest corners of tropical jungles. It is difficult for us, today, to understand the emotion a new species must have aroused, half-glimpsed in the undergrowth, after weeks of trekking in territory where no European—and frequently no human being—had ever trod. It must have been akin to what Sappho's lovers felt when stricken by the dart—a thumping of the heart, tightening of the throat, and sudden tears. Some were rewarded with fame, others only with discomfort, hardship, and death. Who can imagine what Warscewicz felt when, at some point on the Ecuadorean Cordillera, on the slopes of the Chimborazo massif, he spotted, from a great distance, the first *Psychopsis krameriana* (*Oncidium kramerianum*)? Who knows at which precise spot on the Amazon the young Reiss was shipwrecked during his search for *Bollea violacea* (*Huntleya violacea*), which grows on an island midstream?

These were the explorers who brought back the first germs of that obsessive and chronic fever that came to be known as orchidmania. It reached its height in the middle of the nineteenth century and continued at least until the turn of the twentieth. With the passage of time, attitudes toward these plants changed. Initially they represented lushness and mystery, miraculous mirages of tropical forests, with a frisson of savagery in the exotic. Then, with the century, they began to be tinged with fin de siècle associations, living symbols of exclusive preciousness and privilege, and a voluptuous, perturbing sensuality.

Then the scale of the operation changed. Commercial greenhouses appeared, and with the new understanding of the orchid, its cultivation and reproduction, orchids became available to a wide, middle-class market. Europe had come a long way since 1833, when, in England, the duke of Devonshire experienced love at first sight with a flowering *Psychopsis papilio* (*Oncidium papilio*), thereby sparking orchidmania. It was to cost him fabulous sums to acquire the increasing number of new species that he crammed into his orchid harem. The world was moving imperceptibly closer to the day in 1913 when the suffragettes—who took a dim view of orchids and orchidmania—besieged Kew's orchid houses and destroyed more than fifty rare species. Their gesture epitomized the orchid's association with the old patriarchal order, a vegetable version of aspects of society they were eager to overturn.

The First World War then arrived and buried more than orchidmania, with the lives of a generation and their dreams disappearing in the trenches. In the changed social climate of the postwar years, orchids, too, became more democratically shared among the classes. Orchidophiles today can be counted in their millions, as varied as any group of people can be.

What, though, is the state of the orchid today? Their habitats and not theirs alone are severely compromised, the extinction of species gathers momentum. Even toward the end of the nineteenth century, whole colonies of plants were destroyed by unscrupulous hunters keen to keep supply low and demand (and prices) high. In later decades the delicate ecological balances orchids require were seriously altered by deforestation and intensive agriculture. The orchid has paid a high price for its entry into society and civilization.

Nowadays, orchids are grown in greenhouses, protected from the vagaries of the weather, pampered in golden cages with ideal temperature and humidity, tended by an army of enthusiasts who spend every waking hour in their nurture, hybridization, and worship. Nevertheless, despite all these years in captivity, one instinctively knows that the orchids have never become truly domesticated like other plants but remain part of another, savage and independent world, a universe we can only dimly perceive.

This, their recent history, is like the tip of an iceberg, with the greater part of their long saga hidden from our view, spent over millennia far from the eyes of humans. In the following pages we discover whence they came and how they came to us, the many uses to which they have been put, and the curious stories from which the folklore of orchids has arisen.

Chapter 1

Myths and Legends

Today, the exotic orchid is more familiar than at any time in its past. The mystery that once cloaked and protected these elusive plants has been dissolved by travel, science, and horticulture. We can barely begin to imagine how the tropical species must have astonished Europeans when they first set eyes on them two centuries or more ago. Strange, spectacular flowers, they could be larger than life or precious, perfect miniatures, uncannily imitating any number of animals or even evoking the human anatomy.

Their very roots are unearthly. The long, fleshy roots of epiphytic species, for example, choose not to bury themselves in the ground for nourishment but to snake around the branches of trees, or swing, sus-

Drawing by Lady Jane Grey of Groby of an animated scene depicting orchids as fantastic creatures, from Bateman, *The Orchidaceae of Mexico and Guatemala*, back of plate 40

The appearance of *Cattleya labiata* in Europe at the beginning of the nineteenth century caused a great sensation, from *Paxton's Flower Garden*, volume 1, plate 24

pended, over the void as if by magic—curlicues of questions to which no answers are forthcoming. To compound the curiosity they must have engendered, these orchids produced a singular, single fruit—a pod filled with impalpable white powder that dissolved into the air at the slightest breath of wind. The subsequent discovery that this dust cloud was actually a myriad of tiny seeds that refused to be coaxed into germination did little to dispel the original aura of mystery.

Tropical or exotic orchids may have made their first appearance in the West during the Enlightenment, but they proved far too exotic, and of behavior far too complex, to find ready purchase in early eighteenth century rationalism. To this should be added their exuberance and a heavy, sensual beauty that seemed to bear witness to some original sin. Their origins too were remote—lands barely accessible, frequently nameless, of which little was known. Aberrant intruders, orchids were harbingers of primitive, uncivilized people whose customs incited as much anxiety as curiosity. They hinted at worlds still undiscovered, imagined corners still unknown. When the first Europeans arrived in the tropics, accustomed to man-made landscapes and a Nature tamed by their own hard toil, the tropical jungle, teeming with savage animals and seething with sinister rustlings, must have been more awe inspiring than we could possibly imagine. Many people believed unshakably in plants able to devour humans, and in a century hungry for the exotic, rumors of vampire orchids found ready credence. In San Salvador, it was said, orchids were the flowers used to decorate the altars of human sacrifice.

No tale fired the imagination more than that told by an Australian explorer who, pressing on through a nearly impassable area where other adventurers before him had disappeared, at some point came across a long-abandoned native cemetery. Bad weather had brought buried remains to the surface, and the traveler was confronted by the bizarre and chilling sight of an orchid clinging to a human skull. The terrified adventurer saw this as proof of the plant's diabolical nature, and the European press lost little time in taking up the story. The offending orchid was almost certainly an epiphyte, readily adhering to any organic, porous surface. Doubtless it had grown innocently enough from a seed that had drifted into the skull cavity. Speculation continued to increase, however, and contemporary newspapers carried reports of the skull and its accompanying orchid going under the hammer at a London auction. The darkest suspicions thus seemed to find final confirmation.

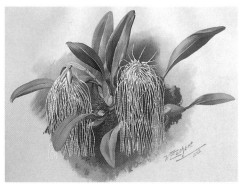

Bulbophyllum medusae, with its heavily scented flowers, was discovered in the Indonesian Archipelago and introduced into Europe about 1840, from Sander, *Reichenbachia*, volume 2, plate 11

Dracula chimaera, syn. *Masdevallia backhouseana*, was discovered by Benedikt Roezl in the forests of the Cordillera in Colombia, from Sander, *Reichenbachia*, volume 1, plate 1

The Myth of Orchis

European orchids have spawned numerous fables, many of them inspired by the two linked and rounded tubers typical of the genera *Orchis* and *Ophrys*. Ancient Greece was the first recorded culture to account for this curious characteristic in myth.

Giambattista Piranesi, *The Retinue of Bacchus*, bas-relief on marble vase, 1778

The legend of Orchis tells of a passionate youth, the son of a nymph, from whom he received beauty, and of a satyr, who added the gift of a robust libido. During a celebratory feast for Bacchus, Orchis committed the sacrilege of attempting to rape a priestess. In submitting to unbridled lust, Orchis had reverted to an animal state alien and repugnant to Greek custom and culture. Because, perhaps, of his privileged birth, he had foolishly imagined himself immune to the Fates, who would swoop to punish any hubris. Punishment being tailored to the crime, his came naturally enough from the animal world into which he had sunk— Orchis was torn limb from limb by wild beasts. Destiny was thus fulfilled, justice done, and the natural and social order re-established. Myth now had nothing to lose by conceding a little generosity. At the intervention of the gods, the youth's body metamorphosed into a modest and slender plant—the antithesis of the frenzied remains that had generated it. With poetic justice, however, the organs of Orchis's undoing were transformed into the plant's nether regions, its tubers. These were fashioned to resemble the very parts of his anatomy that had brought Orchis to grief. The hapless youth's name came to signify not only the plant into which he had mutated, but also the testes. As a botanical name, *Orchis* still applies to the genus of tuberous, terrestrial herbs of which, in myth at least, Orchis was the progenitor. It is also the root of the word orchid and of Orchidaceae, the family to which all these remarkable plants belong.

The Legend of Venus

Cypripedium calceolus is an exquisite orchid, long known in Europe by the name Venus's slipper. One day Venus, the Roman goddess of love and beauty, was out hunting with Adonis when they were overtaken by a tremendous thunderstorm. Venus and her beloved took shelter. Naturally enough, they also took full advantage of their enforced intimacy, and this led to Venus's mislaying her slipper. When the storm had passed, the slipper was spotted by a mortal who immediately went to pick it up. Before he could touch it, Venus's slipper was transformed into a flower whose central petal, the labellum or lip, was not only shaped like a slipper but retained the color of the gold from which the goddess's priceless shoes had been made.

Sometimes ancient myth surfaces in modern science. Searching for a scientific name for the Venus's slipper orchid, the Swedish botanist Carl Linnaeus recalled the tale of Venus and her mislaid shoe. The name *Cypripedium* is derived from Cyprus, Venus's sacred island, and *pedilon*, meaning slipper. The epithet of the first-named species, *calceolus*, is the diminutive of the Latin

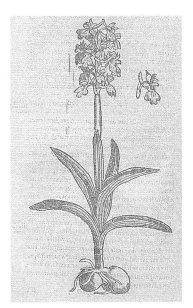

Orchis in flower, from Dodoens, *Florum*

Giulio Romano (?), *Venus Pricked by a Thorn*, engraving by Marco Dente, about 1516

Cypripedium calceolus, from Dodoens, *Florum*

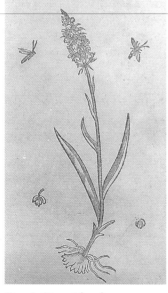

Dactylorhiza with palmate root tubers, from Dalechamps, *Historia Generalis Plantarum*

calceus and means "little shoe." Echoing this idea more than a century later, Ernst Hugo Heinrich Pfitzer placed the Southeast Asian slipper orchids in *Paphiopedilum*, a name combining Paphos, an island with a temple devoted to Aphrodite, with *pedilon*.

Other Legends

If a vein of sensuality runs through the legends of the Mediterranean, those of central and northern Europe are considerably darker, even sinister. The northern imagination has fed primarily on those orchids whose plump, fleshy tubers are surprisingly similar to the human hand. Desire and amorous adventures here give way to the drama of mortality. The plant's own life cycle and perennating organs are read as symbols of death and transfiguration. In Bohemia, the palmate tubers of certain orchids are known as the "hand of death," or the "hand of the dead virgin," symbols in folklore of the hand of a virgin who cried such desperate tears over the tomb of her dead brother that God transformed her into a plant.

In the Tyrolean Alps, legend has it that a young girl allowed herself to die of grief at the unfaithfulness of her suitor. In this case, too, God saw fit to turn her into an orchid, the light-colored, younger root tuber representing the hand of the faithful girl; the darker, older tuber the hand of her unfaithful lover.

Resembling a human hand, the palmately shaped root tubers of European orchids have long been associated not only with passion and sensuality, but also with stealing. Several tales recount the theft of religious works after which the culprits quite simply vanished, while their sacrilegious hands became transformed into tubers, buried deep in the earth in guilty concealment.

In one such tale a monk, for reasons best known to himself, stole an arm from a statue of the infant Jesus, little knowing the price he was to pay and how jealous a God he worshipped. While wandering through the mountains, he strayed from his path and became hopelessly lost, only finding time to bury his treasure before dying of exposure. Legend narrates that the following year, on that very spot, there sprouted a plant that bore the likeness of a child's hand secretly among its roots.

Dactylorhiza maculata with palmate root tubers, from Fuchs, *De Historia Stirpium*

Sri Lanka

In climates warmer than those of Bohemia and the Tyrol, passion once again asserts itself as the major theme in orchid mythology. In Sri Lanka, the former Ceylon, for example, an ancient story tells of a prince who fell madly and unrequitedly in love with his half-sister. Despite his ardor, he resolved to abide by the girl's refusal. The very next day, however, he happened to taste the tubers of *Ipsea speciosa*, a terrestrial orchid with golden yellow flowers that grew in profusion on the island. From that mo-

Forest in Sri Lanka, from Kerner von Marilaun, *Natural History of Plants*

ment, the prince knew no peace and ultimately killed his half-sister in a fit of rage. Ever since, *Ipsea* has been viewed with interest and suspicion in Sri Lanka, where it is still sometimes collected and used as an aphrodisiac.

New Zealand

New Zealand gives us what is perhaps the most poignant orchid myth of all. The Maoris held that orchids were not earthly in origin, believing rather that they were created directly by the demiurge. At the beginning of time, the only visible parts of our planet were the snowcapped peaks of the very highest mountains. From time to time, the sun melted a quantity of snow to create spectacular waterfalls. These, in turn, became rivers and streams, running through valleys and down to the sea where clouds were formed from rising vapor. This cloak of cloud spoiled the sun's view of the earth. One day, the sun resolved to puncture it. The result was a splendid rainbow spanning the whole sky.

When the rainbow appeared, its dazzling color attracted the immortal spirits, who rushed from every corner of the sky to stare, dumbfounded, at the earth, which revealed itself wondrously at their feet. Unable to contain their joy they sang out. Their celestial choir attracted ever more ranks who perched on the creaking rainbow until it finally gave way under their weight and shattered into myriad sparkling fragments. The spirits looked on in ecstasy as colored diamonds rained upon an earth that until that moment had known only the unrelieved browns,

New Zealand, Lake Rotorua seen from Tikitere, from Rowan, *A Flower-Hunter in Queensland & New Zealand*

greens, and blues of bare earth, flowerless vegetation, and wild sea. Every part of the earth waited to receive a precious scattering of rainbow. Caught by the branches of trees as they floated down, these fragments of celestial color were transformed into epiphytic orchids.

The Tropical Forests

One legend from the tropics illustrates how the popular imagination, when fired by these flamboyant plants, has woven fables to account for what we would now consider meat for biologists—as, for example, when seeking to explain the epiphytic habit of many orchids.

When the earth was still very young, the jungle's more aggressively colonial plants set out to terrorize delicate blooms like orchids. Some of the plants managed to stand their ground, quite literally, and defend a patch of land on which to grow. Others, the orchids, grew fragile and etiolated, producing seeds that grew smaller and smaller, dwindling finally to dust.

This sad state was noticed by the gods of the winds who offered their assistance, taking the minute seeds into the sky and showering them on the forest canopy. The great trees pitied these poor defenseless castaways and made room for them, standing aside to allow them the light, air, and space necessary for survival. Terrified, however, by the dizzying heights from which they had been cast, the newborn plants clung by their roots to the branches of their benefactors. In this way, the jungle canopy gradually became populated by these

Angels and flowers, seventeenth century, from Jameson, *Sacred and Legendary Art*

Oncidium limmingbei or *Psychopsis limmingbei*, grasping a tree, from J. Linden, *Lindenia*, 1885, volume 1, plate 20

Epidendrum ibaguense, syn. *Epidendrum radicans*, José's orchid, from Warner and Williams, *The Orchid Album*, volume 4, plate 165

new arrivals, who finally felt at ease in their new habitat.

Costa Rica

The most ancient form of orchid myth-making (where the supernatural explains how a flower came to be, or acquired its shape or color) recurs even in relatively recent times, as, for example, when the world of orchid fantasy hybridizes with more local and human concerns. An instance of this dates from the conquest of the New World.

A young Costa Rican native named José spent much of his time cultivating a small garden in the grounds of a chapel that housed a finely wrought golden cross. Using their favored methods of persuasion on the native people, the conquistadors came to hear of this crucifix and set out to seize it. At the chapel they found José, whom they ordered to hand over the cross. José refused and darted away to the vault of the chapel. Snatching up the treasure, he squeezed through a small window and ran off. Some distance away, cut and scratched after a headlong dash through rocks and scrub, José slowed down, convinced that he had outrun his pursuers. But a few drops of blood betrayed him, leaving a trail for the conquistadors. The heavens, legend tells us, were watching over the righteous.

Flora herself decided on a plan of action—she cast a spell, transforming the drops of blood into a carpet of scarlet orchids that she scattered in all directions to put the pursuers off the scent. Sadly, no one thought to tell José of his salvation. When he turned and saw the men on his heels, he was overcome with fear and died of shock. At that moment each of the miraculous red blooms was transformed into a minute cross, commemorating the youth's sacrifice. They were *Epidendrum ibaguense*, a reedy, scrambling orchid with masses of orange-red to scarlet flowers whose lip is three-armed and cross-like. In many examples of this species, the identification with Christianity is even more inviting as the lip is strongly crucifix-shaped and held uppermost, that is, heavenward.

The Legend of the White Orchid

A youth named Juan was once ordered by his queen to search the forests of South America for exotic flowers, and rare orchids especially, to decorate her palace. The search proved dangerous and difficult. Many weeks later, delirious with fever and close to death, Juan arrived at a village. The villagers gave him refuge in their tiny church and took care of him as best they could. When he regained consciousness, Juan was amazed to see a spectacular white orchid growing on a cross on the church roof. He begged the priest to let him have it, but was firmly refused.

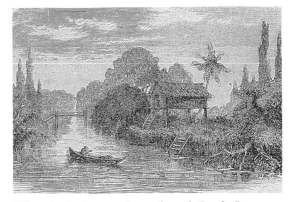

The priest explained that during a terrible famine that followed a long drought, the villagers had begun to waver in their Christian faith. To win the villagers back from paganism, the priest promised that the rains would

Village in the Amazon forest, from de Puydt, *Les Orchidées*

Cattleya skinneri, discovered by George Ure Skinner in the forests of Guatemala around 1830 and often used by the natives to decorate their huts, from Bateman, *The Orchidaceae of Mexico and Guatemala*, plate 13

Cattleya skinneri var. *alba*, from Warner and Williams, *The Orchid Album*, volume 3, plate 112

come only if they donated their most precious possession to the church. Convinced, the villagers brought him a splendidly colored orchid that they had taken from the altar of their pagan gods and now bound to the church cross. No sooner was this done than the sky darkened with clouds and the rains started. Still stranger to relate, once the storm had passed, the villagers saw to their amazement that the rain had washed all the color from the orchid's petals, which now shone pale and ghostly as the moon.

Realizing how difficult it would be to obtain the plant, Juan resorted to guile. He devised a plan where, in exchange for the orchid, he would offer the villagers the one thing they most wanted in the world—victory over their neighbors in the annual, intervillage cockfight. Juan set out for Mexico where by chance he had once been apprenticed to a champion cockfighter. When he returned to the village, Juan was carrying one Fuego de Oro, a magnificent fighting bird and a surefire winner.

The day of the tournament dawned and the two contenders were cast into the pit. For a while they observed each other cautiously, then flew headlong into attack. They were soon enveloped in a cloud of dust. When the fight abated and the sun finally managed to illuminate the pit once more, the outcome of the fight became clear—victory for Fuego de Oro. Now, as the victor preened and smoothed his bloody and disordered feathers, all color, stains, and soiling seemed miraculously to vanish and his plumage shone with the same snowy purity as the coveted white orchid.

Of course, all of these stories are legends. But truth often assumes unexpected guises when filtered through the imagination. For example, it is the case that *Cattleya skinneri* var. *alba* has always been prized by certain tribes in tropical America, and that some peoples (once converted) did establish these orchids on chapel rooftops, thus grafting the pagan spirit of the forests onto the body of the Christian church as a sort of pantheistic insurance policy. So it was that, sometime around 1870, the great orchid hunter Benedikt Roezl became the first European to capture a specimen of *Cattleya skinneri* var. *alba*, which he found growing on the roof of a chapel in Totonicapán, Guatemala.

Chapter 2

From Prehistory to History

Prehistory

To PINPOINT the exact moment at which the Orchidaceae were born involves traveling back in time to the obscurity of prehistory. "Moment" is, of course, misleading—the orchid and its world were the results of long geological eras of complex processes, adaptations, and relationships: real if unrecorded phenomena that are in all probability destined to remain unknown.

Any chance of finding the smallest trace of orchids in rock sediment was significantly reduced by a number of factors, including their preference for humid, tropical areas where decomposition is swift; their soft or grassy tissues; the epiphytic habit of many species; the fact that orchid pollen is transported not by the wind, but by insects; and lastly, the powder-like insubstantiality of the seeds—all of which has meant that orchids have been immensely successful in covering their tracks.

There always will be researchers, however, who refuse to leave a stone—literal and figurative—unturned, and several discoveries regarding the orchid's distant past have been of great botanical and historical importance. The first of these investigators was an Italian, Abramo Bartolomeo Massalongo (1824–1860). He discovered fossils in the Eocene limestone deposits of northern Italy's Mount Bolca with sufficiently orchid-like characteristics to be considered possible progenitors. Accordingly, Massalongo named these *Protorchis monorchis* and *Palaeorchis rhizoma*.

The most interesting work after Massalongo's was that of Adolf Paul Carl Straus. In geological strata of the late Pliocene epoch in Willershausen, Germany, Straus discovered traces of three species that he considered distant but direct orchid relatives: *Orchidacites orchidioides*, *Orchidacites cypripedioides*, and *Orchidacites wegelei*. He also advanced the somewhat controversial hypothesis that the ancestors of these terrestrial species were epiphytes. This theory had its followers but never managed to supplant the consensus that opted for its opposite—evolution from terrestrial to epiphyte.

The earliest substantial evidence of orchids is relatively recent in geological terms, Rutger Sernander (1866–1944) and others having discovered on the island of Gotland, Sweden, some twenty species from the Quaternary period. These are the oldest known close ancestors of the living orchids, a fact that makes Orchidaceae, for all its size, diversity, and distribution, one of the youngest plant families of all.

Antiquity in the East

China

The orchid is first spoken of in Chinese literature, where it has figured constantly from antiquity to the People's Republic. China has no fewer than a thousand indigenous orchid species, but those most commonly encountered in Chinese literature and painting belong to the genus *Cymbidium* and are characterized by long and graceful leaves that arch and curve in the wind like blades of grass. Their flowers are small and subtly colored but elegantly shaped and beautifully poised. Much of their reputation, which spans millennia, is owed to their uniquely delicate perfume.

Early references to plants that are clearly orchids can be found in one of the major texts of Chinese literature, the *Shih Ching*, or *Book of Poems*, from the dynasty of the western Chou (about 800 B.C.). This mentions a plant that is in all probability *Spiranthes sinensis*. *Li Chi*, or *Memories of Rites*, contains references to plants that are almost certainly orchids, as does *Shên-nung Pên Ts'ao Ching*, the *Herbal of the Mythical Emperor*, from the Han dynasty (from about 207 B.C. to A.D. 220), which alludes to both *Dendrobium moniliforme* and *Bletilla striata*.

Ideogram *lan*, Chinese for orchid, from *Chieh Tzu Yuan Hua Chuan*

It was the founding father of Chinese thought, Confucius (551–479 B.C.), however, who first celebrated the orchid for its special qualities, and awarded it primacy in the pantheon of plants. What particularly attracted him was its gently insinuating perfume. Understated yet pervasive, its fragrance symbolized for him the virtuous and the wise, who make their presence and superiority felt while never seeking to oppress others.

Ancient Chinese sources make most frequent mention of three orchids in particular, *Cymbidium goeringii*, known as *shan-lan*, *Cymbidium ensifolium*, *chien-lan*, and *Cymbidium floribundum*, *hsia-lan*. The symbolic value of these three orchids is clear in the various positive epithets that tend to accompany their appearances in classical Chi-

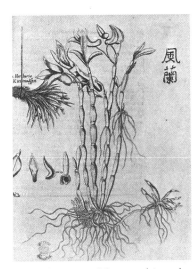

Dendrobium moniliforme, cultivated in the Far East even in ancient times, from Kaempfer, *Amoenitatum Exoticarum*

nese texts: *lan-hui*, good teaching, *lan-you*, intimate friend, *lan-chang*, good harvest, *lan-hsin*, refined woman, and so on.

In antiquity a number of other names for these orchids were in use, such as *ni* and *chien*. It was only when *Cymbidium* began to be cultivated by persons of rank and culture that the name *lan* was used exclusively for orchids. Two of the most exquisite and widely grown Chinese orchids, *Cymbidium ensifolium* and *Dendrobium moniliforme*, can be identified with some certainty in *Nan Fang Ts'ao Mu Chuang*, or *Account of the Flora of the Southern Regions*, the first Chinese manuscript entirely dedicated to botany, written about A.D. 300 by Chi Han, Emperor Hui Ti's minister of state. So large have orchids loomed in the literature, herbalism, and fine art of China ever since that one would need a time scale as generous as Chinese culture's own to account for each appearance.

Around the first millennium the earliest works dedicated exclusively to orchids and orchid growing began to appear. Many of these have been lost, but those surviving include Chao Shih-kêng's *Chin Chang Lan P'u*, published in 1233, describing some twenty different species and their cultivation, and Wang Kuei-hsüeh's *Lan P'u*, or *Treatise on Chinese Orchids*, published in 1247, which describes thirty-seven

One of the ancient entrances to Beijing, from I. L. Bishop, *Chinese Pictures*

The island of the pagoda on the Min River, from Fortune, *Three Years Wandering in China*

different kinds. While these works give some idea of the importance of orchid cultivation during the Sung dynasty (960–1279), it is nearly impossible to describe the extent of the orchid obsession and the massive, if not mass production of books, essays, drawings, and treatises on every aspect of the plant that has been a constant in Chinese history, blossoming along the huge stretch of time from antiquity to the Long March.

Japan

From continental Asia the Chinese term *lan* set sail for the islands of Japan where it became *ran*. Here the first mention of the orchid is in the ancient tale of an emperor's wife who, after years of sterility, managed to give birth to thirteen children in succession after deeply inhaling the inebriating perfume of *Cymbidium ensifolium*, known in Japan, poetically if predictably, as thirteen great treasures, or *ju-san-tai-ho*.

But it was not until 1758 that a work devoted entirely to our plants would appear in Japan: *Igansai-ranhin*, written by Jo-an Matsuoka under the pseudonym Igansai and pub-

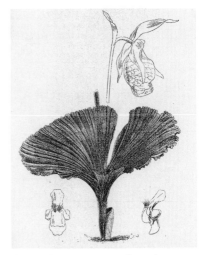

lished in the reign of Cheng-te although commissioned by the previous emperor Higashiyama. This work, especially when enhanced by the detailed text and splendid illustrations of the 1772 edition, did much to fill centuries of silence. For its wide range of species and sound good sense it has seldom been bettered, and is still a valuable practical guide to the cultivation of temperate eastern Asian orchids today.

The paucity of literature before the eighteenth century is by no means an indication that the Japanese were not interested in orchids. Members of the genus

Cypripedium japonicum, from de Puydt, *Les Orchidées*

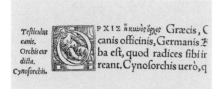

Cartouche for Orchis, showing the Greek mythological character who gave orchids their name, from Fuchs, *De Historia Stirpium*

Calanthe were widely grown at least a century before, as were *Bletilla* species and the cymbidiums so beloved of the Chinese. One of the most highly prized Japanese garden plants is the *fuh-ran*, or orchid of the winds, *Neofinetia falcata*. This is a small monopodial epiphyte with graceful foliage and delicately formed, pure white flowers. Like so many of the orchids to have captured the hearts of Japanese gardeners, it is native to that country, where it was at first grown only by samurai and the nobility. Meanwhile, the imperial aristocracy was growing *Dendrobium moniliforme* as a particularly luxurious air freshener, its perfume filling the rooms of the court.

Other Sources in Antiquity

Other parts of Asia fail to make more than vague and sporadic reference to orchids, and it is difficult to establish precise references in the classical literature of the continent. A number of scholars, however, have rooted out orchids in Sanskrit texts of the Aryans of the Indian subcontinent, in the *Rig-Veda* and *Atharva-Veda* (1550–1000 B.C.), for example. Similarly optimistic eyes have recognized orchids in the *Papyrus Ebers* (about 1660 B.C.) and in Assyrian herbalist literature of the era of Ashurbanipal (668–627 B.C.).

Antiquity in the West

Theophrastus

Orchids first took root in the Western imagination with the myth of Orchis and its luxuriant offshoots and elaborations. The next, more scientific stage came in the work of the philosopher-botanist Theophrastus (born about 372, died about 286 B.C.), a native of the island of Lesbos who worked closely with Aristotle and followed him as head of the Athens Lyceum.

Theophrastus discusses plants, probably *Ophrys* and *Orchis*, in relation to sterility, describing their two rounded root tubers, *Scilla*-like leaves, and *Acanthus*-like flower spikes. It was Theophrastus who first applied the name *Orchis* scientifically, echoing the myth of Orchis and reflecting the resemblance of the double root tubers to the male genitalia.

Dioscorides

The next Greek to take up the tale of the orchid, quite some time later, was the soldier-herbalist Dioscorides (flourished A.D. 50–70), born in Anazarba in Cilicia—today, Asia Minor. In *De Materia Medica*, Dioscorides describes two plants similar or possibly identical to those discussed by Theophrastus. Whereas Dioscorides names these plants *Satyrion* and *Serapias*, he also mentions the older name, *Orchis*, and its associations with fertility.

Dioscorides took the identification of the orchid root with human fertility further, espousing the doctrine of signatures under which medicinal plants were supposed to treat most effectively those parts of the human body they most closely resembled. Under the doctrine, the kernel of a nut, for

Engraved title page from Theophrastus, *Historia Plantarum*

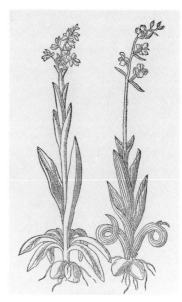

European orchids, from Mattioli, *Commentarii*

example, was associated with the brain, and the orchid with the testicles, potency, and fertility. The doctrine of signatures found favor as late as 1600. Its most famous proponent was Giovanni Battista Della Porta, who in his *Phytognomonica* (1588) attempted to extrapolate the various virtues of plants from their similarity in shape to parts of the human (and animal) body.

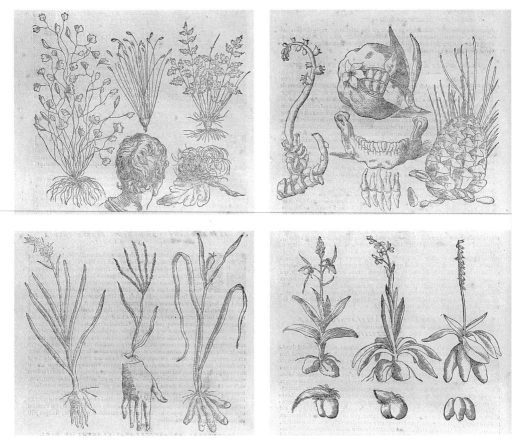

According to the doctrine of signatures, parts of the human body can be healed with plants that resembled them; orchids were associated with the male genitalia and fertility, from Della Porta, *Phytognomonica*

Pliny the Elder

The Romans were certainly well acquainted with the orchids that carpeted, and still carpet, the fields and meadows of Rome and the surrounding country of Latium. Ever playful and associative, the Roman fancy seized on the orchid's appearance and reputation for fecundity, linking it with satyrs and a cast of lubricious gods and demigods in imaginary play throughout the Mediterranean's scrubby maquis and shady groves. Several Roman authors refer to orchids, most notably Pliny the Elder (A.D. 23–79). An acute, perhaps overacute observer of natural phenomena in his *Historia Naturalis*—after all, Pliny's curiosity led to his death in the eruption of Vesuvius at Pompeii—he compiled what Gibbon called "that immense register where Pliny has deposited the discoveries, the arts, and the errors of mankind."

One of the many if minor consequences of the fall of the Roman Empire was the passing of orchids from Roman history. During the Dark Ages, only brief and obscure references to them would appear, and then sporadically, as in the manuscript *Codex Anicia Juliana* (A.D. 512) and the *Codex Neapolitanus* (A.D. 640).

The Renaissance

Along with so much that the ancient world had revealed and that the Dark Ages had obscured, orchids, and plants in general, reappear in the Renaissance. Hieronymus Tragus (1498–1554) was the first exponent of a theory that was to prove oddly persistent in one form or another: that of the similarity between orchid flowers and animals. In its modern form, this theory

Annibale Carracci, *Scene with Faun, Satyr, and Silenus*, about 1597

focuses on the resemblance of orchid flowers to their insect pollinators and makes a plausible, evolutionist's case for mimicry. In the
high Renaissance, the link between orchids and animals was altogether more fanciful. Commentators were, for example, troubled by the apparent lack of orchid seed, the seed of orchids being infinitesimally small and soon dispersed. Hieronymus Tragus interpreted this seeming absence by means of the doctrine of signatures. The flowers of some European orchids resembled birds; moreover, the leaves of others were spotted. Could it be that orchids relied not on seed at all, but sprang up in areas where birds had mated and carelessly spilled their sperm?

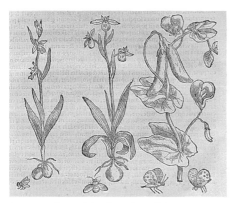

An extension of the doctrine of signatures was the theory that some orchids originated from insects, from Della Porta, *Phytognomonica*

Guido Reni, *Native American Offering Neptune a Container of Seeds to Take Back to Europe*, engraving by J. F. Greuter, from Ferrari, *De Florum Cultura*

Hieronymus Tragus was not alone in this hypothesis. In the seventeenth century he was joined by a Jesuit priest, the erudite German, Athanasius Kircher (1601–1680), author of *Mundus Subterraneus* and a famous treatise on music. For Kircher, evidence to support the theory that orchids were spawned by animals came from shepherds who had observed an abundance of orchids in areas where their animals copulated. This theory was a particularly resilient if convoluted development of the ancients' belief that wasps, bees, and other insects were generated by the rotting corpses of cattle, a belief reinforced for Christian commentators by Judges 14:8, "and behold, there was a swarm of bees and honey in the carcase of the lion." If that was so, the theory went, orchids must surely spring from sperm spilled by whichever animal it is that also gives rise to the type of insect that the orchid flower in question resembles: orchids with plump, bee-like flowers growing from the thick-set bull; those with more slender, wasp-like flowers from the horse; and so on.

The theory had clearly taken purchase in the collective imagination, for all the efforts of the seventeenth century scientist Francesco Redi and others who sturdily opposed it. At the end of the same century Pierre Pomet still included a full-page illustration of bees and lions in his *Histoire Generale des Drogues* (1694). Across the Channel, the English herbalist William Turner (1510–1568) also mentioned orchids in his *Herbal* of 1568, classifying them conventionally within the context of classical texts, as did William Langham in his *Garden of Health* ("1579" but actually 1597). John Gerard (1545–1612), in his *Herball or Generall Historie of Plantes* (1633), described and attempted to classify a good number of species. John Parkinson (1567–1650), pharmacist and herbalist in the reign of Charles I, also consolidated existing theories and, in his *Theatrum Botanicum* (1640) advanced yet another bizarre theory as to the relation between orchids and the sex of the human fetus. Parkinson also made interesting mention of a North American orchid, probably *Cypripedium acaule*, introduced into England by transatlantic settlers and among the very first exotic orchids to be brought to European shores.

The scientific climate was changing,

Charles de L'Écluse, engraved title page from *Rariorum Plantarum Historia*

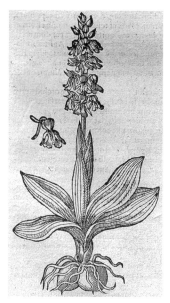

Orchis figured in *Rariorum Plantarum Historia* by Charles de L'Écluse

Leonhard Fuchs portrayed in *De Historia Stirpium*

however. For all that the approach to plants continued to be based on their properties and usefulness, and was still suffused with folklore and myth, it is also undeniably true that toward the late Renaissance there began to grow a purer and more identifiably scientific interest in the vegetable kingdom. In Rome, from the mid-sixteenth century on, the gardens of the aristocracy were becoming, in effect, miniature botanical gardens, with a notable number and variety of species. One outcome of this was the publication of a number of works whose botanical coverage had to keep pace with the new and expanding wealth of garden flora. For example, that of Pier Andrea Mattioli (1500–1577), published in 1554, illustrates and describes orchids with revolutionary clarity and precision.

In the same period the European native *Cypripedium calceolus*, Venus's golden slipper, so celebrated in legend, made its first published appearance in *Rariorum Plantarum Historia* (1601) by Charles de L'Écluse (1526–1609). A Flemish humanist and botanist, de L'Écluse exerted enormous influence over the changing gardens of Europe, not least in his promoting the introduction of foreign plant species.

Although the fast-evolving arts of engraving and printing assisted greatly in disseminating information about Orchidaceae and plants generally, orchids still had to bide their time for a monographic study.

But their presence in gardens, herbaria, and herbals was growing all the time. Ever more species were included in each successive volume—Otto Brunfels (born about 1488, died 1534) of Strasbourg accounted for six orchids among the two hundred species described in his *Contrafayt Kreüterbuch* (1532–1537). This number would increase to eleven species in Leonhard Fuchs's *De Historia Stirpium* (1542). A celebrated doctor at the universities of Ingolstadt and Tübingen, Fuchs (1501–1566) described more than four hundred native European plants and one hundred exotic species.

Modern History

But science would soon hold sway over myth and mystery. From the mid-seventeenth century onward, all new studies, illustrations, and writings tended to be based on painstaking observation and objective statements aimed at something approaching the discipline of botany. Geographically, too, things had changed. In the past, the principal regions of botanical exploration had been Europe, the Mediterranean, western Asia, and to some extent, India and China. Now attention shifted toward the distant, little known tropics and subtropics of America, Asia, Africa, and Oceania. If early modern studies had concentrated on European species, it was now their exotic counterparts that monopolized the attention of experts.

Accademia dei Lincei

At the beginning of the seventeenth century, the Roman nobleman Federico Cesi founded the Accademia dei Lincei, "as a continuous encouragement and reminder to achieve that perspicuity and penetration of the mind's eye which the investigation of all matters requires, and to observe minutely and diligently, both within and without, all the objects which present themselves in this great theatre of Nature."

Coatzonte coxochitl, that is, Stanhopea tigrina, from Recchi, *Rerum Medicarum*

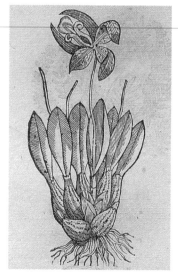

Chichiltic tepetlavhxochitl, that is, Laelia speciosa, from Recchi, *Rerum Medicarum*

One of the academy's first undertakings was the publication in 1651 of *Rerum Medicarum Novae Hispaniae Thesaurus,* the so-called *Mexican Treasure,* an abbreviated version of the work that Francisco Hernandez had produced for Phillip II of Spain, describing and splendidly illustrating the plants and animals of the New World.

The First Modern Students of Botany

Chief among the pioneers of the new direction in botanical studies was Hendrik Adrian van Rheede tot Draakestein (1631–1691), governor of the Dutch colonies in Malabar, southern India, during the second half of the seventeenth century. Rheede managed admirably to combine his administrative duties with his interests as a botanist—he cataloged a range of tropical Asian orchid species in *Hortus Indicus Malabaricus* (1678–1703), a twelve-volume account of Southeast Asian flora containing more than eight hundred magnificent plates, the work of the Carmelite, Father Matteo di San Giuseppe. Each plant is named in Tamil, Arabic, Sanskrit, and Latin.

The late seventeenth and early eighteenth centuries marked the zenith of the Netherlands' colonial expansion. The flourishing Dutch East India Company had established its own network of ports throughout the Middle and Far East. While the propagation of botanical knowledge and the discovery of new floras might not at first have been uppermost in the minds of these explorer-merchants, it was certainly one of the most profitable by-products of colonialism. One of those to exploit the Dutch East India Company's network was Engelbert Kaempfer (1651–1716), a brilliant and courageous German physician. Kaempfer was sent by the company first to Jakarta, then to Java and Japan, where he lived for two years.

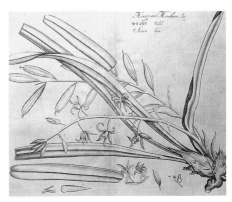

Cymbidium aloifolium, from van Rheede tot Draakestein, *Hortus Indicus Malabaricus*

His enthusiasm for orchids is evident in *Amoenitatum Exoticarum* (1712), in which he described several new Japanese species.

One of the earliest and most remarkable characters to work in and around Indonesia and describe its orchids was Georg Eberhard Rumphius. Born in 1628 in the city of Hanau, Germany, Rumphius was probably of Dutch extraction. A professional adventurer, in his youth he was variously a mercenary for the Venetian Republic, a sailor in the Dutch East India Company, and finally a soldier in the Portuguese army. He then returned home only to set off again immediately for Batavia, now Jakarta, where he was awarded the status of "first merchant."

From this improbable background a botanical passion steadily developed that would become Rumphius's raison d'être. Settling on the island of Amboina in the then Dutch East Indies, he collected and studied the local flora, growing its more beautiful, useful, or bizarre representatives in a small garden near the town hall. Rumphius's obsession with botanizing would also prove his psychological mainstay when, in later years, he was vexed by a series of Job-like trials: the deaths of his wife and daughter in an earthquake; the loss of his sight; the destruction of his garden, herbarium, and papers in January 1687, when fire ravaged the city of Amboina.

Unabashed, Rumphius sought help from the governor of Amboina and a group of assistants and began work all over again. His masterpiece, *Herbarium Amboinense,* was completed shortly after his death in June 1702 and was published posthumously between 1741 and 1755. This great early flora describes 1,200 species, is illustrated with 696 magnificent plates, and runs to twelve volumes, two of which are devoted to orchids. Among Rumphius's many achievements, he was one of the first to posit the presence of pollen in orchid flowers, to recognize their fruit, and to reach the conclusion that the white powder contained in the fruit might well be seed.

Now, at the end of the seventeenth century, the orchid's time seemed to have come. Superstition and myth had receded into the oblivion

Detail of engraved title page with illustration of Georg Eberhard Rumphius, from *Herbarium Amboinense*

View of the island of Amboina, from Rumphius, *Herbarium Amboinense*

of time past, and more and more frequently, men of science were taking a close, impassioned, but analytical look at the plant world.

Carl Linnaeus

The Swedish botanist Carl Linnaeus (1707–1778) is remembered for at least two great achievements. Faced with bewilderingly fast growing numbers of species, he developed a system of classification based on plants' sexual organs that would allow speedy and relatively accurate identification of almost any flowering plant. Confronted with a lawless mass of confused and idiosyncratic plant names, he established firm rules of botanical nomenclature, one of the most important of which demanded that every plant name be binomial, made up of two terms, genus name and species name. The result of Linnaeus's innovations is the radically simple and internationally intelligible method of scientific naming that we use to this day. Linnaeus introduced the binomial systematically in *Species Plantarum* (1753). Perhaps of greater interest to us here is that he named and classified in this work an unprecedented variety of orchids: some eight genera containing sixty species in all.

So much for Linnaeus the botanist. Linnaeus the man was apparently a sociable, likable soul, as fortunate in his profession and university career as he was unfortunate in his private life—possessing, contemporary gossips commented, an untamed shrew of a wife. His botanical forays into the Swedish countryside, surrounded by scholars and students from the whole of Europe, ended in long, convivial dinners and al-fresco dancing.

M. Hoffman and F. Bartolozzi, *Portrait of Carl Linnaeus*, engraving by H. Meyer, from Thornton, *Temple of Flora*

Franz Bauer

In approximately the same period, the great botanical artist and illustrator of plant anatomy, Franz Bauer (1758–1840), was also coming to prominence. Bauer was born in Austria, where his father worked as an artist in the principality of Liechtenstein. Soon after his father's death, Franz decided to break loose and see the world, starting with London. No sooner had Bauer set foot in the English capital than he was spotted by Joseph Banks, who recognized his immense promise and determined to have Bauer for the Royal Botanic Gardens, Kew, of which Banks was the founding director. Banks provided Bauer with a salary and made him Kew's botanical illustrator. Wider fame soon followed, and he was later made drawing master to the "flower" of England's court, Princess Elizabeth.

The work that particularly interests us here is Bauer's *Illustrations of Orchidaceous Plants* (1830–1838). One of the most impressive botanical texts ever produced, it contains drawings of almost all the

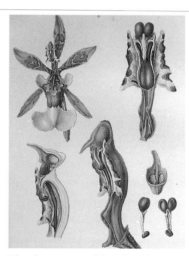

Floral anatomy of *Oncidium baueri*, illustration by Franz Bauer, from Bauer and Lindley, *Illustrations of Orchidaceous Plants*

Galeandra baueri, a native of Central America, named in honor of Franz Bauer, from de Puydt, *Les Orchidées*

exotic orchids then arriving in Europe. With the help of a microscope, which he used with genius equal to that to which he applied the brush and pencil, Bauer pushed forward the frontiers of botany, analyzing plant anatomy and revealing microparticulars that were faithfully reproduced in his illustrations, uniting as no one had ever done before him the exquisite poetry of form and art with scrupulous scientific rigor.

Carl Ludwig Blume

Professional eclecticism was one of the qualities characteristic of almost all the early orchid specialists—most of them had started work in other fields and came to botany through pure passion and any number of surprising routes. A typical example of this phenomenon was the aptly named Carl Ludwig Blume, born in Braunschweig, Germany, in 1796. Blume studied medicine and as a young man went off to Java to exercise his profession.

Blume's curiosity was aroused by the strange and luxurious local flora, not least the opulent orchids, and he was soon working on the *Tabellen en Platen voor de Javaansche Orchideën*, which extended existing floristic studies of the region and subdivided the native orchids into three groups according to the composition of the pollen masses. Interest in exotic plants was at the time so great that Blume received great acclaim, and he returned to Holland where the whole of academia awaited him with open arms and the post of director of the Leiden herbarium.

With ease, ability, and some good fortune, Blume

Phalaenopsis amabilis var. *alba*, from Sander, *Reichenbachia*, volume 2, plate 4; Carl Ludwig Blume established the genus *Phalaenopsis* in 1825

had reached the peak of his profession. He was not, however, to stay there for long. Blume's irascible temper led him to guard his research work jealously and despotically. One by one, institutions and individuals abandoned him, and he was left with the lonely, monotonous perusal of his monopolized field.

Robert Wight

Until this time, Indian orchids had remained, figuratively speaking, in the shade, waiting to be picked and presented to history. This task was ultimately performed with missionary zeal by a young Scottish surgeon, Robert Wight (1796–1872). Wight arrived in Asia under the aegis of the East India Company. He demonstrated such skill and perception in his pastime, botany, that he was soon sent to Madras as director of the Botanical Gardens. We have no idea how good a surgeon he might have made, but his achievements in his new career of botany were prodigious.

Wight's first work was *Illustrations of Indian Botany* (1831). It was followed by *Prodromus Florae Peninsulae Indiae Orientalis* (1839), describing some fourteen hundred local species, and *Icones Plantarum Indiae Orientalis* (1838–1853), the latter the result of years of research and a comprehensive flora of India. Its six volumes, which include orchids from fifty-seven different genera, is finely illustrated with 2,101 plates, many of them the work of Indian artists.

Forest of southern India, from Kerner von Marilaun, *Natural History of Plants*

Australia has always been of great botanical interest, the goal of orchid hunters such as Joseph Banks and Robert Brown, who would collect local specimens and bring them to the West to be studied and cataloged. In the mid-nineteenth century there was renewed botanical interest in Australia, and a new wave of travelers again arrived to build on European knowledge of Australian species.

Ferdinand Jacob Heinrich von Mueller

One of the most important of the new generation of explorers of Australia was the physician and botanist Ferdinand Jacob Heinrich von Mueller (1825–1896), born in Rostock, Germany. His first work was a study of the flora of Schleswig-Holstein, but after seeing one of his family die of tuberculosis, and having become infected himself, he decided on a change of climate.

The decision proved judicious, both for his health and for botanical knowledge. For his first four years in Australia he combed the most remote parts of the outback, collecting and cataloging enormous numbers of plants. His work earned him the position of director of the Melbourne Botanical Gardens. Many of his collections were sent to Kew, to be described in the seven-volume *Flora Australiensis.*

Luxuriant vegetation in an Australian forest, from de Puydt, *Les Orchidées*

Australian forest, from de Puydt, *Les Orchidées*

Dendrobium bigibbum subsp. *phalaenopsis*, one of Australia's most famous orchids, originally named *Dendrobium phalaenopsis* by Robert David Fitzgerald and sent to Europe in 1824, from Warner and Williams, *The Orchid Album*, volume 4, plate 187

A maverick with widely ranging interests, Mueller dabbled in geography, at the same time inventing new measures to improve Australia's economy and industry, not the least intriguing of which was the introduction of the camel as a means of transport. He also had a predilection for titles and honors generally, which he collected from a number of institutions and ruling houses, including a barony from the sovereign of Württemberg.

Robert David Fitzgerald

Another distinguished expert on Australian flora was Robert David Fitzgerald (1830–1892), author of a great monograph on his special passion—orchids. As an adolescent, Fitzgerald's twin callings were engineering and ornithology. He soon built up a considerable collection of stuffed and cunningly mounted birds, complete with eggs. When he moved with his family to Australia, Fitzgerald took up various government posts but continued to add new species to his collection. His road to Damascus occurred in the Wallis Lake area when, on a long excursion with his friend L. S. Campbell, his attention was attracted to a splendid specimen of *Dendrobium speciosum* hanging over the lake from a cleft in the rock. Fitzgerald carefully transplanted it to his own garden, thereby seeding a love of orchids that would grow throughout the remainder of his life and result in the remarkable *Australian Orchids* (1785–1894), which contains his own illustrations.

Harry Bolus

South African orchids had received comparatively little attention until the late nineteenth century, when the career of Harry Bolus (1834–1911) was evolving from that of pioneer-adventurer to botanist and respected academic.

Bolus's start in South Africa was far from promising. Soon after arriving from England he fought as a mercenary—more for food than fame—in the so-called Kaffir War. Next Bolus worked in insurance, but at the same time he also contrived to acquire and run a sheep farm. In a few years he passed from poverty to considerable wealth. During this more leisured phase of his existence, Bolus developed a general interest in the plant world and began a detailed and extensive study of a vast area of South Africa, resulting first in his *Orchids of the Cape Peninsula* (1888), then *Icones Orchidearum Austro-Africanarum* (1893–1913). On his death he left his estate to the South African College, enabling others to engage a passion for plants similar to his own, only from somewhat easier beginnings.

Alfred Celestin Cogniaux

Inevitably, South America is the next stop on our orchid tour. Here one of the names most frequently encountered is that of the Belgian botanist Alfred Celestin Cogniaux (1841–1916). An untiring scientist, Cogniaux was responsible for revising the large and, at that time, rather disorderly field of

Disa uniflora, syn. *Disa grandiflora*, South Africa's most famous orchid, from Sander, *Reichenbachia*, second series, volume 1, plate 15

Brazilian orchids. He documented them in the orchid volume (1878) of the monumental *Flora Brasiliensis* and in numerous shorter botanical works. He is remembered in the orchid genus *Neocogniauxia*, a genus of two species from the Hispaniola and elsewhere in the West Indies, with slender stems and showy scarlet flowers.

John Lindley

With John Lindley we come to the mid-nineteenth century and the height of orchidmania. Newly discovered orchids were arriving daily in Europe at this time in staggering numbers—so far as cataloging them went, chaos reigned. What was needed was an indefatigable organizer and scrupulous scientist who would take upon himself the task of controlling names, eliminating duplication, and reviewing the whole field. The call was answered by John Lindley (1799–1865), the father of modern orchidology.

Lindley's output was prodigious. *The Genera and Species of Orchidaceous Plants* (1830–1840) remains a most comprehensive work on orchid classification. Drawing on the work of collectors, herbalists, and all the available literature, Lindley cataloged and described all the then known species of orchids. This almost superhuman effort coincided with *Illustrations of Orchidaceous Plants* (1830–1838) in collaboration with Franz Bauer, and, lastly, by Lindley's unfinished series of monographs on orchid genera, *Folia Orchidacea* (1852–1859).

George Bentham

One of Lindley's friends and collaborators was George Bentham (1800–1884), described by his colleagues as a reserved, humble, and doggedly hardworking man. Bentham's great contribution to botany was no less than the full-scale reclassification of the plant kingdom. Where orchids were concerned, this entailed Bentham's positing a division of the orchid family into five tribes, each comprising a number of genera. In his magnum opus, *Genera Plantarum*, Bentham with his collaborator J. D. Hooker described the families of all flowering plants. He was rewarded by having two orchid genera named after him, *Benthamia* and *Neobenthamia*.

Charles Darwin

Science still had a lot to say on the subject of orchids, however, and used as its mouthpiece that most famous of naturalists, Charles Darwin (1809–1882), who posited and gave his name to the theory of evolution by natural selection. Darwin's own evolution is a struggle for survival in miniature, decidedly bad school reports giving way to half-hearted attempts at careers before his embarking on scientific research.

The event that changed the course of Charles Darwin's life was, famously, his five-year-long voyage on board H.M.S. *Beagle*. The

Charles Darwin's grandfather, Erasmus Darwin, set the Linnaean system of classification to verse in his phenomenally successful poem, *The Loves of the Plants* (1789), a few lines of which speak specifically of orchids:

> With blushes bright as morn fair *Orchis* charms,
> And lulls her infant in her fondling arms;
> Soft plays Affection round her bosom's throne,
> And guards his life, forgetful of her own.
> So wings the wounded deer her headlong flight,
> Pierced by some ambush'd archer of the night,
> Shoots to the woodlands with her bounding fawn,
> And drops of blood bedew the conscious lawn;
> There, hid in shades, she shuns the cheerful day,
> Hangs o'er her young, and weeps her life away.

Charles Darwin taking a walk in the country, from Holder, *Charles Darwin*

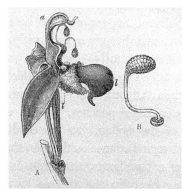

Ophrys apifera, from Darwin, *On the Various Contrivances by Which British and Foreign Orchids Are Fertilised by Insects*

An orchid house by James Bateman at Knypersley, England, from Bateman, *The Orchidaceae of Mexico and Guatemala*

eventual, published outcome of that voyage is known well enough. Among Darwin's other activities, however, his smaller studies, and notably those of orchids, gave him particular satisfaction, writing that no subject had ever interested him so much in his life as the orchid. It took Darwin's rare powers of observation and deduction finally to understand the complex mechanisms of orchid pollination, described in his book, *On the Various Contrivances by Which British and Foreign Orchids Are Fertilised by Insects.*

The story goes that as he was strolling in the Devon countryside, Darwin would observe the curious dances insects performed around orchid flowers. From these observations, he inferred and eventually proved that the plants specifically attracted the insects, which were then used as pollinators.

James Bateman

One of the orchid's more colorful chroniclers was James Bateman (1811–1897), whose personality and range of interests exemplified the vein of eccentricity that ran through many of the gentleman-amateur biologists of the nineteenth century. His garden at Biddulph Grange was myth and masterpiece in its own lifetime, a synthesis of what were then thought to be the best of the canons of style, with rockeries, trees, and avenues creating contiguous but separate gardens. Thus a dark, difficult path led to the hidden Chinese garden, followed by the Egyptian corner, extensive rhododendron plantations in imitation of Bhutan and Sikkim, a pinetum, and an arboretum.

Bateman's love affair with orchids started early. He is said to have been made to stay behind after school to copy out half the book of Psalms as a punishment for lateness. Young Bateman's (unsuccessful) excuse for his tardiness was that he had stopped at a florist's window to covet and then purchase a plant of *Renanthera coccinea*.

One of the many advantages of Bateman's immense personal wealth was that he could employ field collectors, such as Colley, who explored so tirelessly in Central and South America. He was also in easy contact with

Stanhopea tigrina, described for the first time by James Bateman in 1837 after obtaining it from John Henchman, who gathered it near Xalapa, Mexico, from Sander, *Reichenbachia*, volume 2, plate 15

the academic world. John Lindley, who detested the dandy in men of Bateman's sort, nonetheless admired his scientific zeal and was moved to name an orchid after him, *Batemannia colleyi*, democratically including the collector's name. Bateman was also fortunate in meeting George Ure Skinner, an intrepid orchid collector particularly active in Guatemala and thereabouts. Through Skinner, Bateman was able to build up one of the most important collections in England. It is this, and his eccentric but exquisite study, *The Orchidaceae of Mexico and Guatemala*—in so gargantuan a format as to make no more than one 125 copies feasible in its first print run—that more than justify Bateman's place in the pantheon of orchid pioneers.

All Bateman's personality, wit, culture, and scientific nous emerge in the plant descriptions and cultivation notes of *The Orchidaceae of Mexico and Guatemala*. In addition to fascinating topographical and ethnological drawings and some cheeky vignettes (by, among others, George Cruikshank), Bateman also provided forty superb color plates, including one of the first cultivated odontoglossums.

Heinrich Gustav Reichenbach

The mid-nineteenth century produced two of the most celebrated and tireless researchers and orchid experts of all times, both German. The first, Heinrich Gustav Reichenbach (1824–1889), from Dresden, had already proved promising when, as an eighteen-year-old, he helped his father with his *Icones Florae Germanicae et Helveticae*, drawing at least fifteen hundred plants. It was his own three-volume monograph on orchids, however, *Xenia Orchidacea* or *Beiträge zur Kenntniss der Orchideen* (1854–1900), together with numerous successive works, that earned him the title of Orchid King.

Such was his scientific prestige that, as professor of botany and director of the botanical garden at Hamburg, Reichenbach could command the attention of collectors and orchid experts the world

Vignette from, and caricature of, James Bateman's voluminous tome, *The Orchidaceae of Mexico and Guatemala*

over. All that we know of him is that he worked maniacally for and on his orchids, dedicating himself to them body and—considering his will and testament—soul.

Reichenbach had always been somewhat mysterious, so it was not a complete surprise when he bequeathed his herbarium, library, and instruments—a botanist's treasure trove—to the Vienna Natural History Museum, but on condition that it be conserved in sealed cases that were not to be opened for twenty-five years. If the museum refused, the legacy was to be offered to Uppsala, then Harvard, then Paris, on precisely the same conditions. Vienna accepted.

Ernst Hugo Heinrich Pfitzer

Another important orchid expert of the late nineteenth century was Ernst Hugo Heinrich Pfitzer (1846–1906). A Prussian from Königsberg, at twenty-six Pfitzer was already professor of botany and director of the botanical garden in Heidelberg. He held that botanists had been too dependent on the structure of the flower in forming classifications and positing theories of orchid evolution. Pfitzer concentrated his research on the foliar parts.

Hybridization

The beginnings of artificial orchid hybridization were faltering for a number of reasons: techniques for artificially pollinating orchids were discovered relatively late in the West (about 1850, whereas the Japanese appear to have been hybridizing orchids in the eighteenth century); the extraordinary variety and novelty of existing orchid species made the need to "invent" new ones nearly redundant; and there were problems of understanding posed by the complex structure of the orchid flower, and the plant's sexual and reproductive processes. An advantage of this late start, however, is that orchid hybrids artificially created in Western cultivation have been chronicled like those of no other plants.

Paphiopedilum Morganiae, a hybrid of *Paphiopedilum superbiens* and *Paphiopedilum stonei* (see Plate 13) created by John Seden, successor of John Dominy in the English nursery Messrs. Veitch, and published in *The Garden* in 1883, from Warner and Williams, *The Orchid Album*, volume 7, plate 313

The Manchester clergyman, William Herbert, was the first to force the hand of Nature, describing in *On Hybridization Among Vegetables* (1847) his early experiments with different species of orchids. Robert Gallier was making similar progress in 1849, but both were foiled by the problems of making orchid seed pods ripen, and the seeds themselves germinate.

A few years later another attempt was made, this time by John Dominy (1816–1891), foreman at the famous Royal Exotic Nursery owned by the Veitch family. Guided by John Harris, an Exeter surgeon and amateur botanist, Dominy successfully crossed *Calanthe masuca* with *Calanthe triplicata*. The plant flowered in 1856, and John Lindley named the first artificial Western orchid hybrid to flower *Calanthe* Dominyi (*C. masuca* × *C. triplicata*) in honor of its raiser. Dominy had also made an experiment in 1853, crossing *Cattleya guttata* with *Cattleya loddigesii*, but it is unclear whether this cross succeeded in that year. What is known is that the result of this parentage, *Cattleya* ×*hybrida*, did not flower until 1859.

The impact of Dominy's work was immense, to the extent that his disciple, John Seden (1840–1921), had created five hundred artificial hybrids by the end of the century. Ever since, regular bulletins have announced new hybrids, with the year of registration, the names of their parents, and the breeders. Little more than one hundred years after the first cross, the total number of registered artificial orchid hybrids had increased dizzyingly to 110,000.

Chapter 3

Patrons and Hunters

Eᴛxoᴛɪᴄ orchids entered the Western consciousness in the second half of the eighteenth century. At first, their advent caused subdued interest, then growing curiosity, before finally erupting, with the ever increasing welter of species, into the delight and delirium of nineteenth century orchidmania. Only tulips in the seventeenth century had known a similar if shorter heyday, when the Sublime Porte opened to release them from the lands of the great sultan onto an unsuspecting Europe.

Exotic orchids arrived in Europe at a propitious moment, an epoch pulsing with an appetite and admiration for exotic flora. They represented the fascination and loveliness of far-off lands that were fast coming closer as colonialists built up the

Orchids at an international exhibition of the 1890s, from L. Linden, *Les Orchidées Exotiques*

Victorian greenhouse for exotic plants, from a private archive

great empires of the nineteenth century. It was in such conquered territories that orchids were uprooted or stripped from trees and rocks, beginning their long journey to hothouses and herbaria. The Low Countries were the first to import them, from the Malay Archipelago, followed by Spain and Portugal from Central and South America; Great Britain from India, China, the West Indies, and West Africa; France from Madagascar; and Belgium from Africa.

A new breed of pioneers began to roam the globe in search for new orchids to hunt down, gather, and send home. Often they entrusted their booty to merchants, ships' captains, pirates, or colonial civil servants—anyone remotely likely to guarantee the plants' safe passage to Europe.

This phenomenon had some effect on the life of society—unlikely alliances were forged, the aristocracy playing an essential role in sponsoring research, financing expeditions, and, with their collectors' mania, keeping up the commercial value of orchids. As patrons, the aristocracy became linked to an odd assortment of scientists, mavericks, and solitaries—people who turned their backs on the secure conventions of the Victorian and Edwardian eras, choosing instead long periods of privation, danger, and exploration in faraway forests.

Many were the knights of adventure who underwent unimaginable trials and suffering and whose promising careers were cut short. More than one gave his life to the capture of an unknown species. This is the beginning of the orchid's heroic period, an epoch when men lost their heads, quite literally, over a rare plant from which no obstacle smaller than death itself could deter them. This is the epic phase in the orchid's history, written in the sweat and blood of a

Waterfall in a greenhouse re-creating the humidity of the tropics, from a project by Dillwyn Llewellyn in *Gardener's Chronicle*

Caravan of orchid hunters riding along a mountain path in the Andes, from Millican, *Adventures of an Orchid Hunter*

Orchid hunters in the Cordillera of Marcapeta, Peru, from de Puydt, *Les Orchidées*

Nocturnal scene in the Brazilian forest, from de Puydt, *Les Orchidées*

group of adventurers and explorers—the hunters of wild flowers that could sometimes prove every bit as dangerous as their animal counterparts.

Joseph Banks

First in this roll call of botanical heroes is Joseph Banks (1743–1820). Little in Banks's childhood gave any indication of his future development. His school reports show him to be more accomplished on the sports field than in the classroom. During his years at Oxford he was obliged to quell his budding naturalist's interests, but the death of his father left him in possession of an immense fortune. Rich and free as the air, he immediately left Oxford and took a private tutor, the astronomer and botanist Israel Lyons. From Lyons he acquired the scientific foundation on which he was to build at Cambridge, where he excelled in his new, chosen career as naturalist.

Banks's golden opportunity came when the Royal Society decided to organize an expedition to the South Seas, under the command of James Cook and with Banks as mission director. Fired with energy and enthusiasm, Banks was obsessive in his preparations, picking his staff with enormous care. As a traveling companion he chose Daniel Solander, a former pupil of Linnaeus. To man and equip the ship he used ten thousand pounds of his own fortune, with which he also procured the services of four artists, a staff of servants, and the best equipment available. Writing to Linnaeus, the naturalist John Ellis remarked, "No people ever went to sea better fitted out for the purpose of natural history, or more elegantly."

Benjamin West, *Portrait of Joseph Banks*, 1771

The journey of H.M.S. *Endeavour*, which began on 25 August 1768, was to prove in its many vicissitudes the prototype of many biological expeditions. The ship first anchored off Tierra del Fuego, where the expedition members encountered the rather timid natives, and where the first specimens were picked. The first lives were also culled there when two members of the expedition died of exposure—a fate Banks himself miraculously escaped. With the Americas behind it, the ship then sailed into the Pacific, landing in Tahiti, New Zealand, Australia, and the Malay Archipelago, where Banks contracted and nearly died of malaria. They were then shipwrecked, for good measure, but survived. Three years after setting out, the expedition returned home, considerably the worse for wear but with a considerable cache of orchids to their credit.

Banks continued to prosper. In 1771, George III appointed him royal scientific advisor and honorary director of the newly created Royal Botanic Gardens at Kew. Essentially a pragmatist, Banks hung up his vasculum and immediately set out to make Kew the world's most prestigious botanic garden. In his role as the grand master of botany, Banks sent plant hunters across the globe. Later, he established botanic gardens in Jamaica and Ceylon. Sources record the extraordinary and moving intensity of the briefings Banks held before sending his men off

Joseph Banks and Daniel Carl Solander meet the natives of Tierra del Fuego, from a private archive

New Zealand viewed from the bridge of the *Endeavour*, from a private archive

on what he considered to be true botanical missions. As he listed the dangers and privations they would have to face, Banks exhorted his botanical explorers to make, when called on, the supreme sacrifice for the single aim of adding new species to the sum of our knowledge of the living world.

His words contained an element of sad prophecy—one of his men did indeed die of exposure in North America. On H.M.S. *Bounty*'s infamous mission to take the breadfruit tree to the Americas—one of Banks's pet projects—another died of pneumonia during the desperate forty-seven days aboard the small boat that the mutineers granted to Bligh and those who remained loyal to him.

View of the Australian coast with Cooktown and the Endeavour River, from Rowan, *A Flower-Hunter in Queensland & New Zealand*

Robert Dodd, *The Mutiny on the Bounty*, 1790

Banks, the spiritual father of botany, for forty years president of the Royal Society and one of the founders of the Horticultural Society of London (later to become the Royal Horticultural Society), was a kindly, personable man. During the wars he worked tirelessly for the release of foreign naturalists captured on board various ships, and converted his Soho home into an open house for the world's botanists, and a celebrated center of learning with an extensive library and botanical collection.

Olof Peter Swartz

If Banks was one of the founding fathers of modern orchidology, Olof Peter Swartz (1760–1818) has to be recognized as the first real orchid specialist. Swedish in origin, he was born in the port of Norrköping, at the head of an inlet on the Baltic Sea. Swartz graduated from the university in Uppsala before indulging his botanical passion by traveling the length and breadth of northern Europe and Scandinavia.

Swartz's next step—or leap—was across the Atlantic at the age of twenty-three. He explored widely in North America before making his way to Jamaica, Hispaniola, and the adjacent islands. There he collected numerous species, orchids among them. On his return to Europe, he stopped off in Britain and made a study of British botanical practices and source materials. Back in Sweden, he continued to comb the whole of Scandinavia. During his presidency of the Stockholm Academy, Swartz worked on his *Prodromus Descriptionum Vegetabilium . . . in Indiam Occidentalem* (1788) and *Flora Indiae Occidentalis* (1797–1806) in the latter describing thirteen genera and twenty-seven

Daniel Holm, *Lapland Landscape near Kvikkjokk*, 1869

species of West Indian orchids. Swartz continued to work up until his death in September 1818.

Louis Marie Aubert du Petit-Thouars

In this same period an extraordinary figure, the Frenchman Louis Marie Aubert du Petit-Thouars (1758–1831) was living a life of adventure—and poverty—in various parts of the world. The first we hear of him is during the French Revolution when he was imprisoned for two years. To celebrate his freedom he fled to the islands of Mauritius, where he busied himself preparing a map of the region. Next he moved to Madagascar, living, as ever, impoverished, traveling inland on months-long excursions, hunting for orchids. He returned to France around 1802 and began to organize the material he had collected with much effort, publishing a series of studies on African orchids, of which he was one of the earliest experts. In 1820 recognition from the Establishment arrived when he was elected a member of the French Academy.

Angraecum in the forests of Madagascar, from Kerner von Marilaun, *Natural History of Plants*

Robert Brown

To Scotland now, to meet Robert Brown (1773–1858), one of the most important orchid collectors and researchers of the eighteenth and nineteenth centuries. The son of a clergyman, Brown set out to study medicine but soon realized that he had little interest in the human body, and considerably more for plants. He gave up his degree course and, with no other means of finance, was forced to join the army, which sent him to Northern Ireland. Here he used his long hours of free time to observe the natural world, collecting and cataloging the plants he came across in the area, including an unknown species of moss. Brown had the good sense to communicate his discovery to none other than Joseph Banks, who, sensing his potential, called him to London. Banks selected Brown to take part in an investigative expedition along the Australian coast on board H.M.S. *Investigator*. Other personnel chosen for the voyage included the botanical illustrator Ferdinand Bauer (brother of Franz), the horticulturist Peter Good, and the landscape artist William Westal.

Australian forest near the Pioneer River, from Rowan, *A Flower-Hunter in Queensland & New Zealand*

The mission left for the Pacific on 19 July 1801, arriving on the Australian coast the following year. In the meantime, an appalling number of its members had died of dysentery—an exorbitant price to pay for an expedition that nonetheless garnered some 3,800 specimens, including many orchids, over its four-year duration.

On arrival at Port Jackson, Australia, the explorers realized that the timbers of H.M.S. *Investigator* were rotting, and that the ship was unseaworthy. While the captain hired another ship, the *Porpoise*, in which to return home with the plant specimens, Brown, Bauer, and a small number of others prolonged their exploration for eighteen months while waiting for their colleagues to return for them. Tragically, the second ship went down in the Torres Strait between New Guinea and Australia, and only a few members of its crew were able to find rescue on board another vessel. The priceless cargo of newly discovered

Dendrobium superbiens, a native of northern Australia, from Warner and Williams, *The Orchid Album*, volume 7, plate 312

plants was consigned to the deep. As if this were not enough, on arriving in Mauritius the survivors of the *Porpoise* were received with hostility by the French governor, who could think of no better welcome than to sequester the boat and clap its wretched captain, Matthew Flinders, in prison for seven years.

Meanwhile, Brown and his companions, unaware of all this, calmly continued their explorations in Australia and Tasmania, collecting a vast number of orchids—almost a quarter of all those native to Australia. When, finally, they realized that they were waiting in vain for Captain Flinders and a new ship, they patched up the *Investigator* as best they could and sailed home, taking with them this second cache of botanical booty.

After this memorable if melancholy excursion there followed years of sedentary calm in which Brown worked as Banks's librarian, becoming one of the world's greatest botanists and specializing, inter alia, in the reproductive biology of the orchid.

The role of patronage was essential in this early phase of discovery of the exotic orchid. Besides the botanical gardens, only the aristocracy could afford to acquire, at exorbitant prices, the rare species arriving in the West and to construct and maintain the necessary greenhouses. The whole undertaking depended on the strangest of bedfellows: adventurers, aristocrats, academics—and orchids.

William George Spencer Cavendish

One of the most notable aristocratic patrons involved in the history of orchidology, and of orchidmania, is William George Spencer Cavendish, sixth duke of Devonshire. A paragon of English nobility, he was nonetheless born in Paris in 1790, and even taken as a baby to the court of Louis XVI and Marie Antoinette. Like many scions of the British aristocracy, he studied at Trinity College, Cambridge. His parents died when he was twenty-one, leaving him the duchy and one of the largest fortunes in the kingdom.

Devonshire's great interest in English drama led to his buying whole private libraries at the cost of thousands of pounds; he also greatly extended the art collection at Chatsworth, which remains one of the finest private collections in the world. The duke also followed the family's liberal Whig tendencies, championing Catholic emancipation, the abolition of slavery, and an end to child labor. In 1832 he presented a bill to the House of Lords for a reduction in the working week. Twice lord chamberlain, and a personal friend of the prince regent, he was one of the outstanding figures of the age. His estate, however, was not altogether blessed—profound deafness kept him from pursuing what would surely have otherwise been a dazzling public career. It was this handicap that gave the duke an introspective bent, leading him toward the solitary pursuits of the collector.

Plants had never particularly interested Devonshire, and least of all orchids. Legend has it that one day in 1833, however, at a flower exhibition, he came across a plant of *Psychopsis papilio* in full bloom. This extraordinary vision so impressed the duke that he at once

Psychopsis papilio (*Oncidium papilio*), from W. J. Hooker, *A Century of Orchidaceous Plants*

Charles Baugniet, *The Duke of Devonshire and His Circle*, 1852

Oncidium cavendishianum, named for the duke of Devonshire, in a field drawing made by the collector Forget and sent to Sander, the great orchid grower

Dendrobium devonianum, discovered by John Gibson in Assam and sent to Chatsworth, where it flowered in 1840, from Warner and Williams, *The Orchid Album*, volume 11, plate 488; the names *cavendishianus* and *devonianus*, commemorating the duke of Devonshire, belong to numerous orchids

resolved to dedicate himself to orchids in all their bizarre beauty. Ultimately, he was to become the president of the Royal Horticultural Society.

By great good fortune Devonshire met Joseph Paxton, then a humble gardener but destined to become very famous in his own right. Paxton entered the duke's service as a very young man. With Paxton's encouragement, Devonshire developed his passion for plants, redesigning the gardens of his many estates. Exotic orchids were still relatively rare in cultivation when Paxton sent a young plant hunter of enormous talent, John Gibson (1815–1875) to the East, with the stated mission of finding the beautiful leguminous tree *Amherstia nobilis*, and any orchid he could find.

Gibson departed with the retinue of George Eden, earl of Auckland and governor general of India, with the purpose of introducing into India as many medicinal plants as possible. Once these plants had been consigned to the Calcutta Botanic Garden, he set out on the hunting trail. Gibson decided to follow the Brahmaputra River and its tributaries, venturing into the heart of Assam, where he discovered and collected more than a hundred new orchid species. These he sent first to Calcutta, thence to England; they arrived safe and well, bringing the duke "enormous satisfaction."

Gibson's journey to Assam and successive expeditions made Chatsworth's the most famous orchid collection in the world. It was Paxton's idea to build an immense conservatory to contain the treasures that John Gibson and his fellow hunters were sending to Devonshire from every part of the globe. Among the orchids whose names honor the duke are *Cymbidium devonianum*, *Dendrobium devonianum*, *Galeandra devoniana*, and *Oncidium cavendishianum*, immortalizing so much enthusiasm, expertise—and expense.

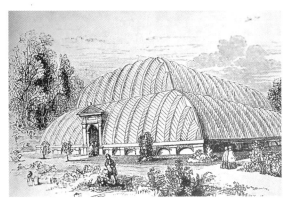

Chatsworth's Great Stove, designed by Joseph Paxton, from a private archive

The Great Stove at Chatsworth, illuminated for the visit of Queen Victoria in 1843, from a private archive

Joseph Paxton

Far from overshadowing his celebrated gardener Joseph Paxton (1803–1865), the duke of Devonshire actually served to increase his fame. Paxton, whose name is commemorated in the orchid genus *Paxtonia* (now *Spathoglottis*), was born into a family of agricultural laborers. He entered the duke's service as a very young man and enjoyed a meteoric rise. Paxton reorganized the vast garden at Chatsworth and built a number of conservatories, one of which, the Great Stove, was the largest structure of its kind ever to have been built at that time, measuring 300 feet in length (91 meters), 145 feet in width (44 meters), and 60 feet in height (18 meters). But Paxton's greatest opportunity arrived when he came first among 240 candidates in the competition to build the Crystal Palace, conceived to host the Great Exhibition of 1851.

Paxton had a passion for orchids, which the duke of Devonshire at Chatsworth was only too ready to share and encourage by financing expeditions and assembling the largest collection of orchids in the world. It is to Paxton that we owe the ingenious solution—still practiced today—of dividing orchid houses into three climate zones —cool, intermediate, and warm—thus replicating the plants' varied natural habitats.

The Crystal Palace, from a private archive

Hugh Cuming

In Hugh Cuming (1791–1865) we encounter one of the most important of the many plant hunters who traveled the globe in an attempt to satisfy Europe's botanical craving. Humbly born in Devon, England, as a youth Cuming was sent to work as sail maker. Here, in daily contact with sailors, tall tales, and the smell of sea air, Cuming's appetite for adventure was whetted. Before long, he sailed for South America where he developed an interest in shells. In search of yet further specimens, Cuming headed into the Pacific and, specifically, to Pitcairn Island, where he stayed with John Adams, one of the last survivors of the mutiny on H.M.S. *Bounty*, which had erupted forty years earlier.

Cuming gathered thousands of shells on his travels, beachcombing the Pacific and dispatching the material to various museums and botanical gardens, although his personal dream was to create a collection of his own in the British Museum. It was on one of these expeditions, to the Philippines, that he suffered a change of heart, transferring his affections to the area's plentiful orchids. With the help of local children, who gave a hand with collecting in jungle areas, Cuming succeeded in sending to Britain more exotic plants than any expedition before. Although barely able to sign his own name, Cuming nonetheless had botanical acumen enough to discover thirty-three new orchid species. He died in London, exhausted by a lifetime of hardship but surrounded by his splendid collections. He is commemorated in *Bulbophyllum cumingii*, an intriguing little orchid discovered in the Philippines with cartwheels of yellow flowers stained with purple-pink and fringed with yellow lashes.

Phalaenopsis in the Philippine jungle, from Burbidge, *Gardens of the Sun*

Rossioglossum grande (Odontoglossum grande), discovered by George Ure Skinner in 1839 and described by him as the loveliest orchid in Guatemala, from Bateman, *The Orchidaceae of Mexico and Guatemala*

Epidendrum stamfordianum, discovered by George Ure Skinner in Guatemala and brought to Europe in 1837, from Bateman, *The Orchidaceae of Mexico and Guatemala*

George Ure Skinner

Another resourceful adventurer and plant hunter was George Ure Skinner (1804–1867). Son of a Scots clergyman, Skinner steadfastly refused to follow his father's vocation or in any way consider an ecclesiastical or academic career. The call he heard was from the world of Mammon and big business, which, however, he resolved to place at the service of his most serious love—botany. Skinner was sent to Guatemala, where between conducting his business affairs he discovered orchids and, with a neophyte's passion, spent days collecting them in the jungles of Central America, finding nearly a hundred species new to cultivation.

After thirty-four years of wandering in the forests, Skinner's thoughts turned once again to Europe. But before returning home to settle down with his collections, he decided to undertake just one more expedition—his fortieth Atlantic crossing. Fate decided differently. In Panama at the very end of his last trip, Skinner fell ill on the eve of his departure. He died within two days, a victim, like so many of his brother plant collectors, of yellow fever. *Barkeria skinneri, Cattleya skinneri, Lemboglossum uro-skinneri*, and *Lycaste skinneri* go some way toward ensuring his immortality.

With some individuals it is difficult to decide whether orchids were the fulfillment or the curse of a lifetime, whether theirs was a mission with a guiding principle or an ill-starred passion that would exact the highest price.

David Douglas

One such star-crossed individual was David Douglas (1799–1834), one of many men who, had they not followed their dream of plant hunting and sacrificed their lives for botany, might well have poured their anarchic energy into an outlaw's existence. A gritty and resolute Scot, he became a fearless, formidable plant hunter. He traveled throughout North America, sending large numbers of plants back to Britain. On one trip he was shipwrecked and lost the fruits of long months of work.

Finally Douglas decided to return to Europe for good. He set sail, stopping over in Hawaii in the hope of finding a few last, possibly unknown species. There he appeared to have vanished until his body was found some days later inside a deep pit dug by hunters. It was mangled by a wild bull that had fallen inside with him. The inquiry that followed threw little light on Douglas's demise. Did he fall? Was he pushed? What became of the scanty funds he had with him? The only witness was his small dog, his faithful companion and fellow adventurer, sole survivor of this last quest, and the only one to return to Britain safe and sound.

Friedrich Martin Josef Welwitsch

The destiny of Friedrich Martin Josef Welwitsch, while not tragic, was marked by hardship and misfortune. He was born in 1806 in Carinthia, Austria, to a family of rich landowners. On coming of age, however, he quarreled violently with his father when he refused to study law; his allowance was stopped, and Welwitsch was forced to leave the university. He kept himself by writing theater reviews, at the same time discovering an interest in botany, which he began to study alone. As soon as he had sufficient means he again enrolled at the university, graduating in medicine.

Welwitsch was beginning to find Austria claustrophobic when he found backing for a botanical expedition to the Azores and the Cape Verde Islands. He left Vienna in the summer of 1839, never to return. Misfortune dogged him immediately. For reasons still unknown, he was arrested on arrival in Lisbon and although subsequently released was not allowed to leave the country. Making a virtue of necessity, he dedicated his "free" time to collecting and cataloging the local flora. Welwitsch became so involved in this project that, when finally granted his freedom, he insisted on staying on in Portugal to finish his research. His reputation traveled as far as the government of Queen Maria II, who sent him on a botanical mission to the Portuguese colonies in West Africa. He left the Iberian Peninsula in August 1853 and traveled to Angola, where he stayed for a couple of years studying the local plants at great personal cost in terms of fevers, scurvy, and leg ulcers.

Welwitsch's discoveries, however, were considerable, and included *Lissochilus giganteus*, now known as *Eulophia horsfallii*, an orchid of extraordinary proportions, whose leaves can grow to 5 feet long (1.5 meters) with the stem as high as 10 feet (3 meters) and the inflorescence 20 inches (0.5 meter) with some twenty pink and purple-green blooms. It was the largest and most magnificent orchid discovered to date and brought Welwitsch considerable fame. He might have stopped there but con-

Eulophia horsfallii, syn. *Lissochilus giganteus*, discovered by Friedrich Welwitsch, from Warner and Williams, *The Orchid Album*, volume 10, plate 457

tinued for a full seven years more, extending his research into central Africa and finally taking more than sixty species of orchids back to Portugal.

But the natural place for a botanist was London, not the Iberian Peninsula. It did not, however, prove the natural place for Welwitsch, who was never completely integrated into British botanical circles, although his scientific reputation was never in doubt. Rumors began to circle that he was living a life of luxury, the direct consequence of which was that a periodic allowance from the Portuguese government was stopped. As a result, Welwitsch found himself in considerable hardship and turned in on himself, an irascible loner. He continued to work tirelessly until a fire damaged not only his house but part of his enormous collection. The nervous breakdown that followed ended only with his death in 1872.

Karl Theodor Hartweg

The career of Karl Theodor Hartweg (1812–1871), from Karlsruhe, Germany, is a halcyon period of calm after the storms suffered by other collectors. An intrepid and indefatigable plant hunter, Hartweg possessed both great good sense and intuition. He conducted years of successful expeditions in Central and South America, earning fame as the collector of the greatest number of orchid species in the first half of the nineteenth century. Exhausted and travel-weary, he returned to Germany and lived out his days as director of the wonderful garden of Schwetzingen in what is now Baden-Württemberg, Germany, where he died.

Odontoglossum crispum, discovered by Karl Theodor Hartweg in 1841 in the Colombian Andes, from Sander, *Reichenbachia*, volume 1, plate 2

Cattleya warscewiczii, from Sander, *Reichenbachia*, volume 2, plate 7

Psychopsis krameriana (*Oncidium kramerianum*), discovered by Józef Ritter von Rawicz Warscewicz on the slopes of Chimborazo in Ecuador, from J. Linden, *Lindenia*, volume 6, plate 246

Józef Ritter von Rawicz Warscewicz

In the early nineteenth century a Polish figure enters the orchid pantheon: Józef Ritter von Rawicz Warscewicz (1812–1866). His earliest adventures were anything but botanical. A fervent political activist, he took part in the Polish Revolution. When it failed, he fled Poland, seeking asylum first in Berlin, then Guatemala. It was there, in the American tropics, that Warscewicz came into contact with the exotic orchids to which he would dedicate his life, and huge quantities of which he sent directly to Germany, bypassing Britain's voracious botanic gardens. After some time in Guatemala, Warscewicz started to travel widely in Central America, accompanied only by native guides and living for years at a time in villages along the route. The Panama expedition, during which he also climbed Chiriquí, the volcano now called Barú, produced a particularly large crop of orchids. Next, he traveled to Costa Rica and Colombia where his discoveries included *Cattleya dowiana* and *Cattleya warscewiczii*.

After years of wandering, Europe began to beckon. Warscewicz broke with the mystery and fascination of the South American jungle for the quiet of Berlin, where he worked as Reichenbach's assistant, helping describe and catalog some three hundred species of orchids. Travel was, however, an ineluctable part of his makeup. Only twelve

months later, in 1851, Warscewicz set sail again, this time for
Ecuador. Here he was robbed of everything he possessed, but his
only reaction was to head in the direction of Bolivia and Peru, collecting many new orchid species on the way.

A related part of his makeup, one that eschewed all constriction
and conditions, perhaps underlay his decision to decline the Royal
Horticultural Society's offer of sponsorship. It was only when he
realized he was seriously ill that Warscewicz returned to Crakow,
where he died soon after.

Joseph Dalton Hooker

Another tireless traveler-botanist was the Englishman Joseph Dalton Hooker, long stretches of whose ninety-one years were spent
combing continents. Born in 1817, he was the son of Sir William
Jackson Hooker, first official director of the Royal Botanic Gardens,
Kew, a post to which the younger Hooker would succeed on his
father's death in 1865. His father recognized Joseph Dalton's intel-
ligence and guided him toward the studies
of medicine and botany. Hooker's vocation
for botany was confirmed when he was
invited to join the H.M.S. *Erebus* Antarctic
mission as medical assistant and naturalist.
The expedition lasted four years, during
which time Hooker collected a vast range
of data and specimens subsequently described in a six-volume study, a rather bulky
passport to academia and the University of
Edinburgh.

Like many botanists, however, Hooker
was restless in the laboratory and herbarium, and soon resolved to travel in India and
the Himalayas, regions whose floras were
little known at that time. He journeyed in

George Richmond, *Portrait of Joseph
Hooker*, from a private archive

some style, far from the austere and solitary expeditions of previous plant hunters. As he recounts in his *Himalayan Journals*, his caravan comprised fifty-six people—porters, interpreters of the various local tongues, and a medley of local odd-job men—an entourage that only succeeded in creating every imaginable problem for the young Hooker.

Dendrobium hookerianum, syn. *Dendrobium chrysotis*, discovered by J. D. Hooker in Sikkim in 1848, from Warner and Williams, *The Orchid Album*, volume 9, plate 419

In Sikkim, Hooker found himself embroiled in a local power struggle and was lucky to escape with his life. At last, following an imprisonment by the raja of Sikkim, he was able to set off in search of the Himalayan orchids that waited for him at the end of a few days' climb. This gave rise to one of Hooker's important contributions to botany, a theory of the distribution of plants according to altitude.

Hooker returned to Europe but stayed only long enough to decide on his next expedition—to Palestine and to Lebanon, to admire the wondrous cedars of that name. His focus shifted next to Africa, for Hooker a source of continuing fascination. He traveled extensively, studying and collecting, before decid-

View of the Junnoo Mountains from the Choonjerma Pass, at an elevation of 19,700 feet (6,000 meters), from J. D. Hooker, *Himalayan Journals*

ing that North America's turn had come. Here, too, Hooker traveled and collected widely, but old age was beginning to make inroads on his stamina, and he finally accepted the sedentary life, succeeding his father at Kew, producing scores of books and articles, admired and honored.

The demand for exotic plants was steadily increasing, moving beyond the tastes of the aristocracy and the needs of botanic gardens and into the lives of a burgeoning bourgeoisie. As demand increased, so did supply. The suppliers were orchid hunters attracted by the rumored income to be won from new, rare and precious species. The solitary sagas of scattered individuals gave way to organized professionalism. Among this new breed of orchid hunter were professional profiteers who would inflate the value of their finds by destroying whichever plants they were unable to transport. Mercifully, others maintained their cachet by more scrupulous means: covering their tracks in the field, remaining tight-lipped once home, preserving the mystery that attended their discoveries and with it, the plants themselves.

Buddhist buildings in Sikkim, from J. D. Hooker, *Himalayan Journals*

View of the village of Lamteng in Sikkim, at an elevation of 9,800 feet (3,000 meters), from J. D. Hooker, *Himalayan Journals*

Acacallis cyanea, from Lucien Linden, *Les Orchidées Exotiques*, dedicated to his father, Jean

Maxillaria nigrescens, discovered by Jean Linden in 1842 in the Cordillera of Mérida in Colombia, from Warner and Williams, *The Orchid Album*, 1884, volume 11, plate 511

Jean Linden

Among the scrupulous professionals, Jean Linden (1817–1898) should certainly be included. A native of Luxembourg, he graduated from the University of Brussels and, by the age of nineteen, was already scouring South America, spending long periods in Brazil, Mexico, Cuba, and Central America. His ten years of travel, which took in the Andes of Colombia and Venezuela, produced an impressive total of eleven hundred species. These were regularly shipped back to Belgium. The years were ones of intense hardship, however, for Linden contracted a number of tropical diseases. Once back in Belgium he was content to cultivate and study his orchids, becoming one of the period's greatest orchidologists. He was also expert in covering his tracks, never afterward revealing the sites of his discoveries.

Thomas Lobb

Another collector who jealously guarded his territory was the Cornishman Thomas Lobb (1820–1894). For Lobb, orchid hunting was more an obsession than a trade or a study. Sources recount that he was an extreme introvert whose conversation centered exclusively on the orchid and its ways. In 1840 he left for the Malay Archipelago, where he collected new and rare species in the mountains of Java. After a short rest in England he departed next for northeastern India. Later, his restless questing would take him over the Pacific, as far as the Philippines.

Lobb sent orchids by the score back to Europe. It was around 1850, during one of his more protracted Asian excursions, that he discovered in Assam one of the great glo-

Phalaenopsis sanderiana and *Phalaenopsis ×intermedia*, from Sander, *Reichenbachia*, second series, volume 2, plate 68

ries of the orchid family, the blue-flowered *Vanda coerulea* (Plate 16). In the Philippines, Lobb discovered *Phalaenopsis ×intermedia*, a natural hybrid between *Phalaenopsis aphrodite* and *Phalaenopsis equestris*.

Thomas Lobb's adventures came to an abrupt end when he lost a leg in the course of an expedition to the Philippines. He returned to Cornwall, where he remained for the rest of his life. Other important Lobb discoveries include *Aerides fieldingii*, *Paphiopedilum villosum*, and the eponymous *Bulbophyllum lobbii*—one of the largest-flowered members of a vast genus, its curiously shaped, tawny flowers have a hinged and gently rocking lip.

Charles Samuel Pollock Parish

Our catalog of hunter-gatherers is now joined by a man of the church, the aptly (and amply) named Reverend Charles Samuel Pollock Parish (1822–1897). At first Parish was not the slightest interested in orchids—bryophytes were his true passion. He was sent to Burma as a missionary and, while searching for mosses in the jungle, felt his soul begin to stir for the many spectacular orchids native to the region. He started to collect them, making his first major discoveries in 1859. These included *Cymbidium parishii* and *Dendro-*

bium pendulum (syn. *Dendrobium crassinode*). Disastrously, this first harvest was lost in its entirety in a storm at sea. Soon afterward Parish began to grow native orchids in the mission garden, where more than 150 different species were converted to Christian cultivation prior to being shipped back home.

Parish stayed in Burma for twenty years, acquiring an extraordinary knowledge of the local orchid flora, which he studied in detail and recorded in a series of drawings. It is to Parish that we owe the discovery of such treasures as *Cymbidium tigrinum* and *Paphiopedilum concolor*. A number of his species bear his name, including *Paphiopedilum parishii*, one of the most showy slipper orchids, whose multiflowered stems bear blooms with spiraling, ribbon-like petals.

Benedikt Roezl

The city of Prague produced one of the most intrepid and charismatic orchid hunters of all, Benedikt Roezl (1824–1885), a man whose mystique was compounded by the hook that he wore in place

Paphiopedilum parishii, from Warner and Williams, *The Orchid Album*, volume 2, plate 86

of his left hand, an accoutrement he picked up in place of the hand he lost while demonstrating farm machinery in Cuba. Aged thirteen, Roezl began work as gardener to an important aristocratic estate, gaining wide practical experience of plants. For forty years of his adult life he traveled extensively throughout Latin America, alone, on horseback or on foot, his gift for orchid divining never failing him. Over the course of his career as a collector, Roezl sent eight hundred species to Europe that were new to science, many of which bear his name. As a result of one expedition alone he collected and shipped home eight tons of plants.

For Roezl, this floral bounty never translated into personal material gain—partly because he was so frequently set upon and robbed. He was once attacked by a group of bandits who were about to kill him when, discovering he possessed no more than a horse and a bag of plants, they assumed he was mad. It being bad luck to murder the insane, the bandits fled, pausing only to make the sign of the cross. Surprisingly, Roezl managed to die peacefully in his own bed, by which time his reputation was so great that the kaiser himself attended his funeral.

Hugh Low

Born in 1824 into a family of nursery owners, Hugh Low differed considerably from his fellow orchid hunters in his working methods and way of life. When scarcely an adult, Low departed for the Far East, heading for Borneo. His interest in orchids was matched only by his interest in the native tribes, whom he studied in great detail,

Miltoniopsis roezlii, syn. *Odontoglossum roezlii*, discovered by Benedikt Roezl in 1872 in the warm valleys of the Dagua River, Colombia, "where it rains 360 days a year," and flowering in Europe for the first time the following year, from Sander, *Reichenbachia*, second series, volume 2, plate 69

describing their dress, customs, and languages. Low was always careful to learn the local dialect and this greatly facilitated his botanical research, gaining him information on plants and access to areas otherwise forbidden to outsiders. Low died peacefully in the spring sun at Alassio, Italy, in 1905 and is remembered in the names of some of his most exciting finds: *Cymbidium lowianum*, *Dimorphorchis lowii*, and *Paphiopedilum lowii*.

Paphiopedilum lowii, discovered by Hugh Low at Sarawak in 1846, from Warner and Williams, *The Orchid Album*, volume 9, plate 428

Cattleya eldorado var. *splendens*, from Warner and Williams, *The Orchid Album*, volume 7, plate 310

Gustav Wallis

Born deaf and mute in 1830, the German collector Gustav Wallis did not begin to develop powers of speech and hearing until his sixth year, and then only slowly. Despite these early difficulties, the infant Wallis became a passionate and talented naturalist. His gift served him well when the company for which was working in Brazil suddenly went bankrupt. Stranded, jobless and penniless, Wallis wrote to the Belgian botanist-horticulturist Jean Linden with an offer to collect plants in South America. Linden accepted with alacrity, sending Wallis to the Amazon. He was later sent by the Veitch nursery to the Philippines, with orders to find *Phalaenopsis* species. On his return to South America, Wallis made a number of important discoveries, but two years later, in 1878, he died of dysentery in Ecuador. A number of orchids perpetuate his name, including *Dracula wallisii*, *Huntleya wallisii*, *Odontoglossum wallisii*, and *Oerstedella wal-*

lisii. Among his most magnificent discoveries are *Cattleya eldorado* var. *splendens* and *Cattleya dowiana* var. *aurea* (Plate 4).

William Boxall

Another nineteenth century plant collector who preferred foreign adventure to the potting sheds of his apprenticeship was William Boxall (1844–1910). He set off for the East, landing in Burma, where he discovered a number of new species of orchids. Next Boxall traveled to the Philippines, Borneo, and Java. Subsequent reports arrived, surprisingly, from Central America where Boxall discovered several new orchid species and many already known— these he shipped to Europe in large quantities. One of Boxall's most celebrated discoveries, however, was not a plant but a medium, ground oyster shells, which proved an ideal substrate for live plants in transit. Back in England, Boxall remained active, giving lectures, attending conferences, and entertaining listeners with traveler's tales that he embroidered shamelessly and amusingly.

Cattleya dowiana var. *aurea*, from Sander, *Reichenbachia*, volume 1, plate 5

Phalaenopsis stuartiana, discovered by William Boxall on the island of Mindanao in 1881, from Warner and Williams, *The Orchid Album*, volume 5, plate 237

David Burke

David Burke (1854–1897) was one of the last of a glorious line of plant hunters, an adventurer who met a suitably appalling and dramatic end. He, too, began by working for the Veitch nursery but soon managed to be sent to Borneo, where he collected and brought back a splendid range of orchids. Following this first adventure, Burke cropped up in the Philippines, New Guinea, northern Burma, and Colombia. Finally, he decided to make his way to the Moluccas, where the natives were notoriously unfriendly. It was to prove a fatal decision—Burke's body was found by a German traveler who chanced there, inside a tribesman's hut on the island of Amboina.

Wilhelm Micholitz

Born in Saxony in 1854, Wilhelm Micholitz traveled widely in both the Far East and Latin America, his progress continuously hampered by the revolts and revolutions then shaking these areas. A courageous adventurer, he was wonderfully adept at both discovering orchids and concealing their most densely populated habitats— competition among hunters was fierce. His collections earned him a considerable fortune on the European markets and he was able to retire to Germany in comfort. After the First World War, inflation ate drastically into his savings, and he lived out the last years of his life in near penury, dying in 1932.

With Micholitz we reach the beginning of a very different century, and the end of the era of the great glasshouse and the orchid hunter. By the end of the nineteenth century the whole orchid ethos had changed. Orchid growing was no longer the domain of the privileged few, but rather of the large and wealthy middle classes. Huge, specialist nurseries oversaw the importation and establishment of wild-collected plants. The germination requirements of orchid seeds finally became understood, making propagation easier and plants cheaper. Orchidmania was an era of dreams and adventures— it was to die, with so many other aspects of the old order, less tragically but equally completely, with the outbreak of the Great War.

Chapter 4

Arts and Customs

THE VAST, varied, and nearly ubiquitous orchid family has been present as a theme in human life at various times and for many reasons. The tubers of European and Asian species were used in antiquity for medicines and foodstuffs. They have also figured in religious and magical rites. In the modern age, orchids have played a role in more secular rites—the arts and social manifestations generally. While most orchid lovers and specialists concern themselves with the plants' physical appearance and cultivation, these plants have equally enjoyed a long and complex sociocultural history wherever they have made contact with the human species.

Martin Johnson Heade, *Orchid, Passion Flower and Hummingbird in the Brazilian Forest*, 1875–1885, from a private archive

Literature

As we have seen, orchids have long been present in the literary traditions of the Far East, where they were valued primarily for aesthetic reasons but also gathered a variety of associations that exemplified desirable aspects of human behavior. In the West, their cultural role has been rather more diffuse and symbolic. The earliest Western writings to play host to native orchids reflected their herbal properties. By the time that exotic species were introduced in the late eighteenth century, the arts and the sciences were parting company. Orchids belonged to the latter. That said, the orchid, wreathed in sensuality, rarity, and exoticism, ever mutable and flamboyant, was bound to capture the writer's imagination. What follows is a brief catalog of the orchid's appearances in Western literature.

William Shakespeare

Hamlet may be a play about doubt, but we can at least be certain that some of the flowers in poor mad Ophelia's bouquet were orchids. When the Queen announces the girl's suicide, she describes Ophelia's last moments as she walks toward the stream where she will drown, singing to the "fantastic garlands" she has made herself, "Of crow-flowers, nettles, daisies, and long purples, That liberal shepherds give a grosser name, But our cold maids do dead men's fingers call them." These "long purples" are native British orchids. Exactly which orchids we cannot be sure, for the shepherds' grosser names clearly refer to the globose tubers of an *Orchis* species, while "dead men's fingers" would seem more appropriate for *Dactylorhiza*. This is

John Everett Millais, *Ophelia*

not to say that Shakespeare (1564–1616) was at fault—critics end-lessly tell us he was a country lad at heart—more that folk or vernac-ular generic concepts tend to be a little looser than their scientific counterparts.

John Ruskin

The great English aesthete and intellectual John Ruskin (1819–1900) was attracted to and intrigued by orchids. With puritan zeal, Ruskin spearheaded a movement conferring ethical and religious status on beauty as an ideal—a prime necessity, he considered, in a world sinking into the gray squalor of the industrial age.

Ruskin believed that flowers, like art, are an essential part of the life of the spirit, and one of the most directly ordained symbols of divine beauty. Accordingly, he held that research into plant sexual-ity was tantamount to sacrilege. The orchid, so overtly sensual and bizarre, disturbed Ruskin. Exotic orchids he rejected outright, but he also took issue with native species for their garish colors and insect-like appearance. The very name *Orchis* caused Ruskin pain, but his proposal to change it to something less explicitly sexual met with no success.

Ruskin's attitude was not quite the bowdlerizing stupidity it might appear today. In the mid- and, particularly, late nineteenth century, the vibrant, healthy naturalism embodied by the tropical forests that people had previously associated with orchids was changing. A paradigm shift was underway in cultural aesthetics, producing at one level a move toward decadence and eroticism. The orchid, once an emblem of colonial adventure, scientific investi-gation, and creation run riot, became identified with luxury and artifice. Meanwhile, Ruskin and others more or less united under the name Pre-Raphaelite decided to oppose the superficiality and elegant

Orchis, from Dalechamps, *Historia Generalis Plantarum*

artificiality of the prevailing culture and to recede into a pre-Renaissance world of courtly convention. Through their influence, flowers, as symbols of purity, assumed increasing importance in the arts, although only the "innocent" rose, lily, iris, or wildflower passed muster—the orchid's credentials were decidedly suspect.

Oscar Wilde

It is hardly surprising that Oscar Wilde (1854–1900), champion of decadence and aestheticism, should have had some association with orchids. While he identified initially with the Pre-Raphaelites, making their "pure" lily his own, somewhat ironic hallmark, Wilde's aesthetics were equally influenced by Théophile Gautier and Charles Baudelaire and by later French and Belgian decadents and symbolists whose taste for the subversive and exotic he was quick to assume. For some fin de siècle commentators, the spirit of the orchid was incarnated in the figure of Wilde. In *The Picture of Dorian Gray*, one protagonist possesses an orchid house at his country seat; orchids adorn his London home and the conversation of his visitors.

Cattleya labiata, the favorite flower of Odette de Crécy, from Warner and Williams, *The Orchid Album*, volume 11, plate 497

H. G. Wells

In the same period an orchid became the central "character" of a novella by a very different type of writer, H. G. Wells. Herbert George Wells (1866–1946) was a prolific and varied writer probably best remembered for his works of science fiction. He was also a prominent member of the Fabian Society and a representative of the Anglo-Saxon tradition of the apostle-cum-peaceable revolutionary. "The Flowering of the Strange Orchid" tells the story of a plant collector, a retiring bachelor who discovers an orchid whose wondrous but treacherous perfume makes him swoon. He is saved from death only at the very last moment, by which time the orchid has wound him in its tentacles and is preparing to suck the vital juices from his body.

F. M. White

Another orchid Lorelei is the protagonist in "The Purple Terror" by Frederick Merrick White (born 1859), published in *The Strand Magazine*, in which a young American sailor, having had a steamy affair with a ballerina, finds himself in the Cuban jungle where he falls under the spell of a bloodred orchid. During the day, the orchid is curled around the highest branches of a tree. By night it steals down the trunk and spreads its petals in readiness for whichever poor wretches happen to wander by and constitute its next meal, their bones adding to the ossuary on the jungle floor.

Marcel Proust

If orchids had not existed, one feels Marcel Proust (1871–1922) would have had to invent them. Their ephemeral sensuality, carnal but coy, coupled with their flamboyant but fragile beauty provided him with the perfect symbol for his characters' contemplative decadence. His favored species seems to have been *Cattleya labiata*, the leitmotiv of Odette de Crécy in *Un Amour de Swann*. Orchids are

Orchids and insects, from Dalechamps, *Historia Generalis Plantarum*

worn in her hair, tormented by her fingers, burst from her cleavage, and cover her with their petals. Their perfume pervades the air on the evening that she and Swann cement their love for each other, thereby becoming, in their secret language, the emblem of their intimacy. Replete with sexual subterfuge and elaborate courtship rituals, Darwin's account of orchid pollination fired Proust's imagination. Orchids provided him with ideal ciphers for his subtle narrative games.

In *Sodome et Gomorrhe* loves and alliances change. Again, Proust interconnects and externalizes these changes through flower, insect, and character, describing the glances, movements, and intricate steps preceding the amorous encounter between the Baron de Charlus and the tailor Jupien. Such parallels between human affairs and natural phenomena are one of Proust's favorite narrative devices. In this case, they enable Proust to examine this passion dispassionately and with a naturalist's eye. By appropriating science, Proust frees himself from moral judgments.

Gustav Meyrink

The Gothic atmosphere that surrounded orchids in the culture of northern and central Europe returns in *Orchideen, Sonderbare Geschichten*—orchids, strange stories—by the Prague writer Gustav Meyrink (1868–1932). One story is "Bologneser Tränen," Bolognese tears, the title referring to a kind of unannealed glass, hard but brittle, and thus a parable for a beautiful object that is a mirage, exploding violently and turning to dust. Meyrink describes the orchid—which he has clearly studied in some detail—as a thing of wondrous beauty that encloses and conceals a demon. His novel pulses with sublimely sensual but sinister women who are metamorphosed orchids. Orchids rain from the sky and invade the earth, luring mortals into fleshy chambers of blood and beauty.

Henry David Thoreau

Henry David Thoreau (1817–1862) takes us, gently, far from the jungle and the jugular to the green fields of New England and the shore of the pond where he chose to live in solitude. There he learned to love the slender wild orchids of the area, modest, unshowy, "fair and delicate, nymph-like." He writes of them in his *Journal*, documenting their different colors, the feelings they aroused in him each spring, and their graceful shapes, which could only be discerned by an eye trained in the lonely love of Nature.

Rex Stout

Among his contemporary American authors, Thoreau was as isolated in his love of orchids as he was in his chosen way of life. Disturbed and dismayed by the tropical species, Nathaniel Hawthorne and Herman Melville dismissed them as lewd and luxurious status symbols. Decades later, these "faults" would become the very qualities that endeared orchids to another American author, the crime writer Rex Stout (1886–1944). Stout's creation Nero Wolfe is one of literature's great mavericks. Like so many fictional detectives before him, Wolfe's attitude toward women leaves something to be desired. Unlike other investigators, however, he detests adventure, in fact movement of any kind, preferring to save his love and energy for beer, good food, and orchids. Like many serious orchid growers, Nero Wolfe has three greenhouses: cool, intermediate, and warm. Each day the otherwise immobile Mr. Wolfe ascends to the roof of his New York brownstone (by elevator) to spend upward of four hours in the company of his "concubines," his orchids.

Art

China

In art as in literature, it is the Chinese who have most often depicted the orchid. In no other country has it been drawn, etched, painted, and described as in China. The beginnings of the orchid's diva status date back to around A.D. 1000 when orchids made their delicate entry in Chinese art. Already canonized in the works of Confucius, they were studied in a number of monographs, acquiring particular importance, for a number of reasons, during the Yuan dynasty (1279–1368), especially during its decline. Zheng Sixiao, active between 1250 and 1300, made the orchid an emblem of patriotic values. He lodged it in the national consciousness when he made a drawing of an orchid in black ink, as a symbol of the era when the Chinese had been deprived of their lands.

During the Ming dynasty (1368–1644) the orchid acquired yet further symbolic values. It came to epitomize ideal examples of both sexes: when depicted alone, the exquisitely poised and mannered court maiden; when illustrated in conjunction with

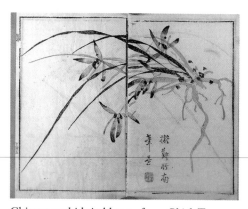

Chinese orchids in bloom, from *Chieh Tzu Yuan Hua Chuan*

Orchids and rocks, from *Chieh Tzu Yuan Hua Chuan*

a rock, the virtuous man, combining strength with sensitivity and elegance.

The painting manual *Chieh Tzu Yuan Hua Chuan* (1679–1701) is a key text in the artistic celebration of the orchid. An exposition of the aesthetic values of the age, the book dedicates a large section to the representation of the orchid, listing the most important artists to treat the orchid in previous centuries in the various genres (many of them nonprofessional writers, and women). Drawing techniques are detailed, concentrating particularly on the leaf, successful depiction of which was held to be the test of a successful artist. Instructions proceed from drawing the simplest strokes, to suggesting a plant animated by the breeze. Each pen stroke and hand movement has its own name, the elements of a genre of Chinese art that has never lost popularity.

Europe

In Europe, the orchid's role as artist's model has been somewhat more pedestrian. Exquisite and faithful illustration of orchids, whether native or exotic, tends to have been the province of the botanical rather than the "fine" artist.

One of the orchid's rare appearances in the Western visual arts is in the unicorn tapestries, seven tapestries in the Metropolitan Museum of Art, New York. Embroidered in the sixteenth century for Ann of Brittany, whose love of flowers is also attested in her *Book of Hours*, decorated with some 350 species, the tapestries are exquisite in their quality of materials, shades of color,

Botanical illustrators at work, from Fuchs, *De Historia Stirpium*

The Unicorn in Captivity, seventh of
the unicorn tapestries

and complexity of composition. Six are perfectly preserved; the seventh is badly damaged in a number of parts. The series illustrates the various phases of a hunt for the mythical unicorn, the gestures of the hunters alternating with glimpses of the animal in a steadily unwinding magic carpet. The tapestry is an allegory of marriage and fertility—only a virgin had the power to capture the recalcitrant unicorn. The unicorn appears, captured within a circular enclosure and tied to a pomegranate tree, in the fragment of the seventh, partly ruined tapestry. The hunt is over. One hundred and one plant species are represented, almost all of which have been identified, although their symbolic connotations are often obscure. In the last fragment, before the shining white body of the unicorn, an orchid has sprung up, probably *Orchis mascula*, traditionally connected with fertility. The orchid is linked with the loved one, the unicorn, and is joined with him inside the flowering enclosure of the family.

Painting

On the rare occasions that the orchid appears in oil painting, it can be difficult to identify. It receives rare attention in Gaudenzio Ferrari's *Madonna and Child*, where a row of orchids in the foreground forms a carpet at the Virgin's feet. Ferrari (1470–1546) was one of the major Piedmont artists, active in Varallo, Vercelli, and Saronno.

Another example appears in *Christ and the Samaritan Woman* by the Veronese artist Girolamo dai Libri (1474–1555), in the Castelvecchio Museum in Verona. The orchid appears with the lily, just behind the figure of Christ. A number of small flowers often taken to be orchids also appear, growing at the foot of the cross, in the disturbing *Pietà* by Cosmè Tura (born about 1430, died 1495), in the Correr Museum in Venice. Both monumental and intimately human, the painting shows huge crosses looming on the horizon of an uncanny, unreal Calvary, against a livid sky. From a tree, a monkey observes the Virgin embracing the body of her son.

Our last artist to immortalize the orchid in oil is the American, Martin Johnson Heade (1819–1904), although his interest is more botanical. In the second half of the nineteenth century Heade organized long expeditions to tropical America to hunt for exotic orchids and hummingbirds in their natural environment. His canvasses throb with the bright and tiny birds in constant movement against huge, stately cattleyas, in romantic landscapes of mist, moss, mystery, and twisted branches.

Gaudenzio Ferrari, *Madonna and Child*, sixteenth century, from the central panel of a triptych originally from the nunnery of Saint Chiara in Milan

Martin Johnson Heade, *Orchids and Hummingbirds in the Brazilian Forest*, 1893, from a private archive

Sculpture

No mystery, however, surrounds the two orchids that grow in stone at Saint Albans Cathedral in Hertfordshire, north of London. In the nineteenth century the cathedral was badly damaged by fire and rebuilt in the Gothic revival style then in vogue. The capitals were decorated with fruit and flowers, including orchids. The cattleya depicted here obviously declares that this decoration is Gothic in its revived form—such exotic flowers would not have been known in Gothic's first flowering. More importantly, the orchids commemorate one of Saint Albans's most famous residents, Henry Frederick Conrad Sander (1847–1920), at whose nurseries more than two hundred orchid species were introduced into cultivation and the great orchid work *Reichenbachia* was composed.

Detail of a capital at Saint Albans Cathedral, a photograph by the author

Magic

Perhaps because of their strange shapes, their apparently unnatural growth habits, or their remote origins, orchids have at various times been co-opted by the occult. In several parts of the world they have been transformed into talismans, amulets, good-luck charms, and whatever else was needed to help destiny take a more tolerable course. The many properties attributed to orchids include the power to ward off evil spirits, improve health, and increase personal worth, courage, and virility. As is only appropriate for plants so strongly linked with sex, orchids have also been considered a vital ingredient in potions for procuring the affections of a loved one.

Love Potions

Southeast Asia and Polynesia are home to *Grammatophyllum*, a genus comprising a dozen or so epiphytic and terrestrial species. One of these, *Grammatophyllum speciosum*, is probably the largest (in the sense of bulkiest, if not tallest) orchid in existence. Its pseudobulbs can reach a height of 10 feet (3 meters), and its inflorescences, bearing hundreds of flowers, a width of 6½ feet (2 meters). The whole plant can weigh at least a ton. The species that interests us here, however, is *Grammatophyllum scriptum*, found in the Philippines, Borneo, Sulawesi (Celebes), the Moluccas, New Guinea, and the Solomon

Grammatophyllum speciosum, from *Gardener's Chronicle*, from Williams, *The Orchid Grower's Manual*

Islands. Each yard- or meter-long flower spike carries some sixty large flowers. These are yellow-green and densely spotted with strange, indecipherable patterns in reddish bronze. It is the seeds of this orchid that spell out the flower's coded messages of love to makers of potions. In the Moluccas, it was believed that adding them to a woman's food would at once ensnare her in a binding web.

Amulets

In tropical and southern Africa grows *Ansellia*, a genus of one, variable species, *Ansellia africana*, commonly known as the leopard orchid because of its dark-spotted, yellow flowers. The genus was named for John Ansell, who discovered the first specimen on the trunk of a palm tree on the island of Fernando Póo, now called Bioko, in 1841. A number of local tribes put this orchid to work making a contraceptive bracelet (short-term in effect, if at all, and for unmarried women only) from leafy parts of the plant impregnated with a paste made from the pseudobulbs. In addition, any bad

Pecteilis susannae, formerly included in the genus *Habenaria*, from a private archive

dreams (connected with spinsterhood, the loss of it, or whatever) could be banished by burning the plant's roots. All in all, the plant was a mini–marriage guidance counsel.

Another genus of interest here is *Habenaria*, comprising some five hundred species of terrestrial orchids that grow throughout America, Africa, and Asia. Many of these are greatly prized by collectors and nurseries for the glowing reds, yellows, and oranges of their flowers—there also exist subtly beautiful pale green blossoms fading into white. Many of these were used by various peoples of the Americas to color their cheeks or dye their weapons, serving the double purpose of scaring their enemies by strengthening their warrior-like tendencies, and ensnaring women by adding a mysterious smile. The same qualities, but differently employed, are invoked by a number of tribes in Papua New Guinea. There, baby girls are wrapped in the leaves of a local species of orchid to encourage the strength, health, and capacity for drudgery without which it is impossible to find a husband.

Evil Spirits

Affairs of the heart have always been a priority for dabblers in the occult, soon followed by the need to keep off or banish the forces of evil. The Chinese answer to problems of the kind was to reach for the nearest orchid. A number of ancient sources testify to the efficacy of orchids in banishing the evil spirits of the forest. The treatise on *Pên Ts'ao Kang Mu* (1590), or *Medicinal Matters*, states that "orchids are used to banish negative forces." The Chinese term for orchid, *lan*, is pronounced exactly like the character designating the idea of shelter, or halting the advance of something or someone. Dioscorides, too, attributed to orchid tubers the power to protect victims of the dark arts.

The orchid's usefulness for exorcisms is described in a number of anthropological sources that speak of a broom made from the pseudobulbs and foliage of *Dendrobium* species and used to sweep the house immediately after the death of an inhabitant. If this is done, death will be unable to return to claim other members of the family. Dendrobiums were also used as protection by certain tribes in the Solomon Islands. Placed on the head, they guaranteed safety when entering unknown or dangerous territory. In other places *Dendrobium* flowers resembling a dog's head

Dendrobium infundibulum, from Warner and Williams, *The Orchid Album*, volume 10, plate 448

are fed to hunting dogs to increase their courage in the chase.

Spells

Yet another species of *Dendrobium* is the subject of a fascinating linguistic phenomenon. In New Guinea, the word *duruagle* denotes both a native species of *Dendrobium* and a woman of easy virtue. Local legend tells of a ghostly young woman who wanders, naked and enticing, along the banks of the region's rivers. Her aim is to ensnare any young men who may cross her path. Should one prove unable to satisfy her doubtless high expectations, he finds himself stricken the very next evening with a cocktail of venereal diseases that only the *Dendrobium* can cure.

Ghosts

In some parts of Indonesia, ghosts were believed to dwell in a number of orchid species. Inhabitants of various parts of Borneo have spun ghostly tales around the genus *Anoectochilus*, small terrestrials whose wonderful velvety leaves are inscribed with arabesques in gold, copper, and silver. Because these orchids grow scattered in the forest's most secret places and can appear somewhat temperamental, vanishing as soon as their habitat is disturbed, legends developed to the effect that they range freely over the jungle, disappearing into thin air in the presence of strangers.

Magic Letters

A close relative of *Anoectochilus*, the Javanese *Macodes petola* takes its name from the vernacular *petola*, which means letter paper. Its leaves are covered in a network of metallic veins bearing an extraordinary resemblance to the script of its native land, so much so that Rumphius adopted the name as long ago as 1750, calling this orchid *Folium petolatum* in his *Herbarium Amboinense*. In the past, juice from its leaves was mixed with other substances and applied to the eyes of anyone learning to read and write. It was recommended particularly for those wishing to become literary experts.

Anoectochilus setaceus, from W. J. Hooker, *A Century of Orchidaceous Plants*

Deadly Potions

Historical sources cite a couple of cases of more sinister potions used in Arnhem Land, Northern Territory, Australia. There, during human sacrifices, the witch doctor would smear his arm with the juice of the pseudobulbs of a native orchid just before killing his victim.

The tubers of some *Habenaria* species, if mixed with other ingredients, produced a potion supposedly able to procure the death of a designated victim. Such sinister uses are extremely rare in the literature, however, the orchid generally being more innocuously employed to wean children, assure the laying quality of hens, discourage slaves from escaping, and other such necessary domestic tasks.

Talismans

There are a number of talismans made of different parts of the orchid and used the world over in various superstitious rites. In India, for example, where snakes are a problem, the only way to avoid their deadly bite was thought to be by carrying around dried pseudobulbs of *Eulophia*. *Vanilla planifolia* was originally used in Mexico as a charm to protect travelers. Back home in central Europe, an old legend narrates how treasure hunters would carry orchid tubers in their pockets. Another proof that Europe was not immune to the occult powers of the orchid comes from Scotland, where a talisman was commonly made from the tubers of *Orchis mascula*.

In Norway, it was believed that the palmate tubers of *Dactylorhiza majalis*, if picked on the Eve of Saint John, would emanate special powers, powers confirmed by the fact that the tubers at that time of year possessed a magically human five lobes—fingers—instead of the usual four. Meanwhile, if the tubers of *Dactylorhiza maculata*

Macodes petola, from Williams, *The Orchid Grower's Manual*

Image of a serpent from Dioscorides, *De Materia Medica*

were buried at the threshold of a house on the same evening, the evil eye would be permanently banished. These and several other tuberous European orchids were long considered to be effective antidotes to witches' spells, particularly spells that produced impotence in men or infertility in women.

Religion

The jungle, the forest, and sweeping fields are where orchids live and flourish. This is the locus of their spirituality, nurtured by perennial contact with the Supreme Being. If removed from their world they will manage to thrive among people, in the greenhouse or the parlor. Before the altar they appear most definitely to droop. At sporadic moments through time, however, among various peoples, orchids have been used in religious rites and have been mentioned in religious writings.

Classical Greece is the first example that comes to mind. There, they were, of course, deemed sacred. Pausanias informs us that orchids were used to weave garlands worn in processions leading to the sanctuary of Hermione, where the faithful performed the rites of Demeter, goddess of harvest and of crops.

Dactylorhiza maculata, from de Puydt, *Les Orchidées*

In China, orchids were embraced with great enthusiasm in Confucian texts, although Confucianism was more a moral doctrine and a vision of cosmic order than a religion. In the regions where Buddhism prevails, orchids are carried even today by the faithful and placed in front of images of the Enlightened One.

Among the pre-Hispanic civilizations of the Americas, civil and religious leaders revealed a quasi-religious enthusiasm for the most splendid orchids available. With the arrival of the conquistadors, this custom was transferred to the Catholic rites imposed on the local cultures. Churches were decorated during baptisms, weddings, and funerals. The altars dedicated to Christ, the Virgin Mary, and the saints were copiously adorned, and the vernacular names of many orchids reveal the religious use to which they were put, or their resemblance to Catholic symbols.

Altar of a Guatemalan church decorated with orchids, from Bateman, *The Orchidaceae of Mexico and Guatemala*, back of plate 13

Epidendrum ibaguense (syn. *Epidendrum radicans*), for example, is known as the crucifix orchid on account of its scarlet flowers, which recall the shape and color of the cross, and the local legend of a young boy who tried to save a crucifix from looters. *Peristeria elata* was called Espíritu Santo on account of the flower's column. The column resembles a dove, a similarity also reflected in its English vernacular name, dove orchid, and in the etymology of its scientific name from the Greek *peristera*, dove. Autumn-flowering *Oncidium tigrinum* is known locally as flor de los muertos and used to decorate tombs and altars on All Souls Day. Other Latin American orchids with local names that date from the arrival of Christianity include *Sobralia dichotoma*, flor del paradíso, a plant that grows to several yards or meters with fragrant, brightly colored flowers, and *Cattleya skinneri*, known in Guatemala as flor de San Sebastiano and used to decorate altars on that saint's feast day.

In Papua New Guinea, adolescents adorn themselves with orchids during rite-of-pas-

Acineta barkeri, formerly included in the genus *Peristeria* and similar to *Peristeria elata*, Espíritu Santo, from Bateman, *The Orchidaceae of Mexico and Guatemala*, plate 8

sage ceremonies marking their entrance into the adult world. Several Indian tribes used bunches of *Cymbidium* flowers to transport them in dreams to the supernatural realm where they hoped to meet the gods face to face.

Medicine

Originally humans used the orchid, very prosaically, for food and medicine. An overview of its medicinal use is curious in itself and an important part of the orchid's overall role in human existence. It has been estimated that of the world's twenty-five thousand orchid species, at least four hundred were used regularly for healing purposes. Very often, the cure was no more than a placebo, but research has suggested that some orchids may contain a number of valuable active principles.

In Europe, for centuries, orchid-based prescriptions recommended by the great Greek and Roman writers continued, with slight variations, to be used in the treatment of a number of ill-

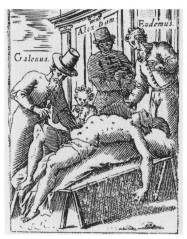

Study of anatomy, detail from the frontispiece of Avicenna, *Canon Medicinae*

The physic garden, from Avicenna, *Canon Medicinae*

nesses. Extract of *Dactylorhiza maculata* was still prescribed in Europe at the beginning of the nineteenth century as a treatment for tuberculosis. Orchids were also used in North America, where various *Cypripedium* species were mixed with spices and used to cure inflammations and skin ailments. Other North American genera, including *Epipactis*, were renowned for treating nervous disorders, and these remedies were later introduced into Europe.

As usual, it was in Asia that the most extensive medicinal use of orchids was made—inevitably, given the continent's remarkable development of natural medicine. Members of the genus *Bletilla* were highly valued in China, Japan, and Tibet for their euphoric and blood-purifying properties.

In China, one of local medicine's most curious surprises is the beneficial use of *Dendrobium nobile*. This plant comes from Southeast Asia and is one of the most widely cultivated orchids. It is known in China by the name of the drug it yields, *shish hu*, and was greatly esteemed in the days of the Han dynasty (207 B.C. to A.D. 220). The essence was obtained from the dried pseudobulbs, and the prescription was so widely used that the plant was farmed for commercial use. It possessed various remarkable properties, favoring the body's yin as well as being an active ingredient for long life. Not least, it was considered an aphrodisiac. Research has shown the presence of numerous alkaloids in this dendrobium, including dendrobina, which causes severe poisoning when administered in large doses.

The spice seller's shop, from Avicenna, *Canon Medicinae*

In Chinese cooking, dishes are important for their curative properties as well as their nutritional value. An example is a dish from southeastern China where pork broth is made with the addition of a local species of *Pholidota*. This genus of epiphytic orchid extends from Asia to Australia; its hundreds of tiny, sac-like flowers are tightly and often spirally arranged on pendulous, chain-like racemes. It is a prized ingredient in a number of recipes, giving dishes a very special flavor; but it is equally prized as an expectorant for allaying asthma. A variety of rice wine, also from this region, is obtained by steeping the pseudobulbs of *Calanthe*. The brew is used to treat a long list of ailments.

The tradition of the Indian subcontinent is quite similar to that of northeastern Asia. Numerous orchids, mainly bearing the name of the extracted drug, feature in the Indian pharmacopoeia. One of the most common in local pharmacology is *Vanda coerulea* (Plate 16). There are also a couple of treatments that ayurvedic medicine calls *jirvanti*, probably distilled from *Coelogyne ovalis*. Farther south, in Sri Lanka, the same term designates an ointment made from other species of orchids, believed effective for treating broken bones and contusions.

Edible Orchid Products

In modern times, people have appreciated orchids for their aesthetic or botanical value. We treat orchids like sacred relics or precious gems, enclosed in glass and wooden cases to protect them from the ravages of climate and time. Orchids were equally coveted by our ancestors. Their passion, however, was based not on admiration for shape and color but on the plant's substance. It was not the orchid's enchanting appearance that whet their appetite, but more concretely, pangs of hunger and the search for food.

In the past, in various parts of the world, a number of plants or parts of plants were used by extracting their essences, brewing beverages from them, or transforming them into products that became immensely popular for a time before slowly declining in fame and then vanishing altogether. All this is now a thing of the past. Our taste for orchids no longer resides on our palates. There is only one product that, despite its waxing and waning in popularity, has persisted obstinately with time, one that we use daily, seduced and satisfied by its aroma: vanilla, a magnificent flavoring produced from the fruit of an orchid.

Vanilla

The peoples of Central America made extensive use of what the Aztecs called *tlilxochitl*, vanilla. Francisco Hernandez, the historian who took part in the Cortés expedition, recorded that it was an essential ingredient for the preparation of *chocolatl*, chocolate. The Aztec emperor Montezuma refused any beverage but this, drinking it fifty times a day from carafes that, tradition fondly imagines, were made of pure gold. The original Aztec term, meaning dark pod, is echoed in its modern, European and scientific equivalents. The term vanilla comes via the Spanish *vainilla* from Latin *vagina*, a sheath or pod.

This new aroma crossed the ocean with the Spanish, then the masters of South America, who introduced it to Europe. Probably among the first exotic orchids to reach the continent, it is difficult to set the exact date for vanilla's arrival although some writers put it at 1510. At first, vanilla was used as a perfume. There are records of chocolate with a vanilla aroma being produced in Spain in the second half of the sixteenth century. After that, however, the essence fell into inexplicable oblivion for many years. There is news of its reaching Great Britain in the eighteenth century but it was officially brought into the country in the year 1800 by the marquess of Blandford. Cuttings were

Illustration from Dufour, *Traitez Nouveau & Curieux du Café, du Thé et du Chocolate*

Frontispiece from Dufour, *Traitez Nouveau & Curieux du Café, du Thé et du Chocolate*

taken to Antwerp and Paris a few years later and were given a rapturous reception. Vanilla's real success story begins there.

From the outset, there were problems in growing the plant. The flowers bloomed but the fruit—the precious pods used to produce the essence—never formed, or the crop proved of inferior quality. Outside their own habitat and without their insect pollinators, fertilization of the plants artificially was long, arduous, and full of drawbacks. Various remedies were sought, including the introduction of some *Melipona* bees from Mexico. All failed. Then, in 1841, Edmund Albius, a former slave from Réunion, discovered a fast, practical method of artificial pollination. From that moment on, the cultivation of vanilla spread rapidly all over the world.

The genus *Vanilla* consists of about a hundred species of orchids that live in the tropics and subtropics. Their habit is liana-like, with long, succulent stems climbing into trees and securing themselves by means of aerial roots. The vanilla of commerce is extracted from the dried, mature seedpods of *Vanilla planifolia*. Today, it is farmed in Mexico, Madagascar, Réunion, and other areas around the equator. *Vanilla tahitensis*, of lower quality, is also worth mentioning, as is *Vanilla pompona*. Pods of this latter species dry very slowly and are used to flavor tobacco in Cuba and in the perfume industry.

When we think of vanilla, our thoughts run to its main use in chocolate and other sweets. But for many peoples, even in Europe, it had a wide variety of other uses, not least medicine, where it appeared in the form of powders, syrups, tinctures, essences, and infusions. Vanilla was used as a stimulant for treating nervous disorders: hysteria, melancholy, impotence, even rheumatism. In some countries, it was also used to control convulsions, menstrual problems, and as a diuretic and tonic.

Fig. 278. — Vanilla

Vanilla planifolia, from Kerner von Marilaun, *Natural History of Plants*

Then there are vanilla's aphrodisiac properties. The records relate that even Montezuma made great use of the essence before going to visit one of his many wives. Europeans soon followed suit, and young husbands and lovers were strongly advised to make liberal use of it. Today, of course, the plant's active principle, vanillin, can be obtained synthetically, although it is certainly not as good as the natural product. Thankfully, this invaluable orchid continues to be farmed, providing its intoxicating essence for those uses—decent cooking, for example—where the synthetic product simply will not do.

Bourbon Tea

Vanilla is unquestionably the most widely used and economically important orchid product but there are still other ways of consuming orchids. One of these was *faham* or bourbon tea from the Mascarene Islands, including Mauritius and Réunion, the former Bourbon. It reached its peak of glory in the drawing rooms of European capitals during the nineteenth century and consisted of an infusion from several types of orchids. Among these was *Jumellea fragrans* (syn. *Angraecum fragrans*) with white, scented flowers. Milk was sometimes added, or spirits believed to enhance the fragrance. It was drunk cold or hot. Bourbon tea was held to be beneficial as a sedative. Oddly, it was also thought to improve one's sense of touch and was often applied as a tincture to the fingertips.

Salep

The most mysterious substance extracted from orchids was unquestionably the elusive salep. Even today it is mentioned in passing, but no more than vague and garbled answers are given as to its true nature. Salep was a substance obtained from the tubers of various terrestrial orchid species. It came originally from the Middle and Near East but was also common in India and parts of China. Brewed from tubers of *Orchis, Dactylorhiza,* and *Ophrys,* salep was particularly popular in Europe during the Middle Ages and, intermittently, even until the beginning of the twentieth century when its popularity faded.

There were variations in the way salep was made in different places but the process was basically a three-part one. The tubers were harvested after the plant flowered, scraped or peeled and then dried in the sun or an oven. The dried product was used to make a flour used in various ways: in milk, water, or broth, as an aromatic flavoring with other spices, in soups, mixed in wine, and so forth. It is still used in some areas of the East. There are salep vendors to be

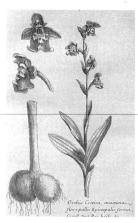

Ophrys cretica, one of the many orchids from which salep was obtained, from Tournefort, *Relation d'un Voyage du Levant*

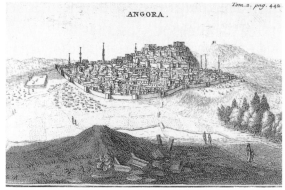

Views of the city of Ankara, the former Angora, in Asia Minor, where salep was quite common, from Tournefort, *Relation d'un Voyage du Levant*

found from Asia Minor to the Balkans, where the substance is stored in large, heated leather bags. It is brought onto the streets by wandering vendors, crying out their wares, and it is listed among the specialties of old Europe in *Larousse Gastronomique*. In the past, of course, European orchids were rather more abundant than they are today, and the custom of harvesting tubers of wild plants correspondingly more widespread.

Salep also had a number of pharmacological uses. It was considered a cure for a variety of ailments, and credited with the ability to release physical energy. Inevitably, as an orchid derivative, the product was also held to have aphrodisiac powers, which might have been due solely to the old doctrine of signatures. Indeed, John Parkinson, in his *Theatrum Botanicum* (1640), even complained that "our pharmacists are wont to adjudge every sort of orchid root an aphrodisiac." Sources narrate how various peoples in Europe drank various beverages at breakfast, including an infusion of saxifraga and salep, apparently sold in taverns and inns. This custom declined and gradually disappeared with the introduction of coffee and tea.

Other Uses in Cooking

Around one hundred orchid species have been used in cooking throughout the world. Some are still in use although the orchid has generally lost its popularity as an ingredient. One example is from Malawi, where markets sell the tubers of a species of *Disa*, a genus that produces some of Africa's most spectacular flowers. When these tubers are cooked and treated, they are an excellent side dish.

Although rarely and only when suffering the pangs of hunger, early colonists of North America fed on terrestrial orchid roots. They had probably observed Native Americans who often used them. One Arizona tribe used orchid roots to make flour. They also extracted latex from tubers to make a natural form of chewing gum. Farther south, Mexico is the native land of *Stanhopea tigrina*, whose magnificent, highly scented flowers were sometimes used to make tortillas.

In India, many parts of *Cymbidium* species—young tender shoots, thick pseudobulbs, and juicy leaves—were used for a variety of dishes.

Australia and Tasmania are places where humans once consumed large numbers of orchids. There, perhaps due to the difficulty of farming the arid land, Aborigines used to harvest the tubers of some of the five hundred species of terrestrial orchids. In the past, many travelers mentioned a concoction called yam, made of orchid tubers, dried and mixed together to make a sweet substance that children adored. A number of species of *Cymbidium* were also used to obtain a kind of meal or starchy powder. Generally, however, the Aborigines would roast their orchids—tubers or pseudobulbs—wrapped in the plant's own leaves.

Chapter 5

The Plant

ALTHOUGH often thought to be exclusive and exotic, the Orchidaceae is one of the largest families—possibly the largest—in the plant kingdom. Approximate estimates put the number of living orchid species at some nine hundred genera containing a total of more than twenty-five thousand species. Given the complexities of classifying so large and diverse a group, and that unguessable numbers of species may still lurk undiscovered, these figures are necessarily imprecise and open to continuous revision. It is certainly the case that scores of new species are added to the list each year, but also that many are lost along with their habitats.

Habitat

There is some justification in the orchid's reputation for exoticism: ninety percent of all orchid species live in the tropics and subtropics. The remaining ten percent, still a sizable number, are spread through varied habitats and territories across the globe. Some orchids flourish on sand dunes, such as *Epipactis dunensis*, others at the edges of the African and Arabian deserts, such as *Eulophia* species. Some seem fond of bare rock; others live hidden underground, the famous Australian *Rhizanthella gardneri*, for example. There are even semiaquatic species, *Malaxis paludosa* (syn. *Hammarbya paludosa*) and some *Disa* and *Habenaria* species, for example.

Two of the most outstanding characteristics of the Orchidaceae are its adaptability, and the manifold survival strategies, patterns, and designs by which the this family clings to life. Like human beings, orchids can cross the limits of space, seeking and stubbornly conquering new lands. Orchids cover a geographic area that ranges from the shoreline to elevations of more than 13,100 feet (4,000 meters) above sea level, from the Arctic Circle, northernmost home of *Calypso bulbosa*, to Tierra del Fuego, where with any luck *Chiloglottis cornuta* can be spotted.

From an ecological viewpoint, most orchids have evolved to occupy what can be a very narrow and precarious environmental niche. In doing so, they usually conform to one or another of four very general habit types: epiphytic, lithophytic, terrestrial, and saprophytic. These are not taxonomic distinctions, or even much of an indication of a species' likely appearance—plants of all sorts and from most of the tribes of Orchidaceae can be found in each of these

View of the dense tropical forest, from de Puydt, *Les Orchidées*

groups—but they do tell us much about the unparalleled evolutionary flexibility of the orchids. More practically, they offer clues to successful cultivation.

Epiphytic Orchids

Many tropical forests are plunged in eternal darkness from which only mighty, Cyclopean trees emerge. The many and multiform epiphytic orchids live in their dizzying heights, winding their roots around branches or letting them cascade into the void. These hanging gardens cover the jungle's upper reaches, producing flowers that, for all that they are hidden and inaccessible, comprise the most magnificent explosion of shape and color Nature has ever produced.

Epiphytes, the word from Greek, meaning "upon a plant," form the largest group within the Orchidaceae. Epiphytic orchids are distributed over a vast area, all but the very driest of the planet's tropical and subtropical regions. In such areas, the dense canopy and understory of vegetation often make the forest floor too dark to sustain much plant life. Unabashed, many of the smaller herbs that one would normally expect to find on the ground have taken to the trees where they perch, making use of the available light, irrigated directly by rainfall, and fed by accumulated detritus and animal droppings. Other plants well known for adopting this strategy include aroids, bromeliads, figs, and ferns. After the bromeliads, however, Orchidaceae is the family that has made epiphytism its own.

Epiphytism is not parasitic behavior; the tree only acts as a support and the epiphytes receive no nourishment from it. Since, at least when growing, epiphytic orchids need abundant atmospheric humidity, they tend

Epiphytic orchid, from L. Linden, *Les Orchidées Exotiques*

to be found more in rain and cloud forests than in open plains and hills. They do, however, appear in scrub and have been known to colonize isolated trees, telegraph poles, even fence posts.

Lithophytic Orchids

Lithophytic or epilithic orchids are very similar to epiphytic orchids in basic behavior, the difference being that they grow on rocks rather than on other plants. These rocks range from sheer cliff faces to the Inca ruins at Machu Picchu and from isolated boulders to rooftops. Like the epiphytes, lithophytes tend to need at least one season of heavy rains and high humidity, although some strongly lithophytic species have evolved a greater tolerance of drought through thicker, tougher foliage, for example. One or two lithophytic species show a distinct preference for the mineral composition of the rock on which they grow, for example, the limestone-loving *Paphiopedilum bellatulum*. That said, many epiphytes can be found growing lithophytically and vice versa. The distinctions are not clear-cut.

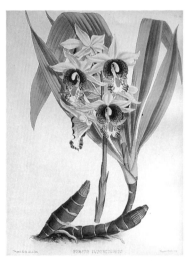

Phaius tuberculosus, a terrestrial orchid, from Warner and Williams, *The Orchid Album*, volume 2, plate 91

Terrestrial Orchids

Terrestrial orchids grow on or in the ground and thus resemble the great majority of plants. In terms of their distribution and diversity, however, they vary greatly. They are found in habitats from the subpolar to the equator. Terrestrial habitats range from meadow to mountain peak and from forest to desert. Among the terrestrials are evergreen and deciduous species with fibrous roots, tubers, tufted growths, cane-like stems, climbing stems, fleshy rhizomes, and pseudobulbs. Almost all orchids from cool temperate climates, as prevail in much of Europe and North America, are terrestrial. Terrestrials from warmer latitudes include members of the genera *Paphiopedilum*, *Phaius*, and *Sobralia*.

Saprophytic Orchids

While the quest for light has driven some orchids to cling to the highest boughs of trees and soaring crags, some have evolved in ways that free them from the pressures of photosynthesis. Saprophytic orchids derive their nutrition from dead and decaying matter. They assimilate nutrients through symbiotic relationships with fungi. Such orchids are fleshy, strangely shaped and colored plants, and usually lack leafy parts and chlorophyll. Species include the ghost orchid, *Epipogium aphyllum*; coral root, *Corrallorrhiza*; bird's-nest orchid, *Neottia nidus-avis*; and violet *Limodorum abortivum*. They are mostly denizens of woodland and forest. Although found in open country, the Australian *Rhizanthella* is even harder to spot than most other saprophytes—it is almost wholly subterranean, scarcely breaking the soil surface with its flowers.

Although the honor is usually awarded to the giant, nonsaprophytic *Grammatophyllum speciosum*, the world's largest orchids belong to the Asian genus *Galeola*. These saprophytes appear as if from nowhere and throw up a mass of climbing, tawny yellow to coral pink stems hung with hundreds of fragrant flowers. The stems can achieve lengths of more than 66 feet (20 meters) in a matter of days, only to wither more quickly than they appeared.

Despite their eerie beauty and enigmatic life cycle, saprophytic orchids are hardly ever cultivated with any success. Their habitats are too specialized, and the symbiotic associations on which they depend for life almost impossible to recreate.

Plant Structure and Behavior

Roots, Rhizomes, Stems, and Pseudobulbs

The spell woven by orchids starts with their remarkable roots. Orchid roots can penetrate the soil or firmly grasp the trunks of trees. They can hang like languid tentacles over chasms in the forest or from baskets in the greenhouse. Nature has given the roots of orchids an elaborate series of functions that they perform spectacularly well.

The plant's development depends on a growth axis that also allows the plant to move. Most orchids are sympodial, meaning that they consist of a rhizome, a serpentine stem that grows continuously, resembling a sort of vegetal centipede. It creeps along, thrusting endless roots outward to anchor the plant in the soil or to the bark of its host tree. The rhizome follows the flow of the seasons—periodically, usually yearly, it lengthens from the tip or sideways. In many cases, the rhizome develops fleshy, swollen stems—these can be spherical, disk shaped, pear shaped, ovoid, flask shaped, cylindrical or reedy, minute or enormous.

Cattleya mendelii, syn. *Cattleya labiata* var. *mendelii,* a sympodial orchid, from Sander, *Reichenbachia,* volume 1, plate 15

The fleshy, swollen stems—pseudobulbs—act like a camel's hump, serving as reservoirs for precious minerals and water, important for survival during long dry spells. For greater protection, the plant also maintains an "eye" at the base of each pseudobulb. These persist long after the pseudobulb has developed, ripened, and flowered. They remain dormant until the plant is severely threatened, or loses its active growing lead, or until the old pseudobulb is detached from the main plant, in which event the eye rapidly develops into a new growth to replace the old. This type of sympodial, pseudobulbous behavior is most evident in such genera as *Cattleya*, *Cymbidium*, *Laelia*, and *Odontoglossum*. Not all sympodial orchids have pseudobulbs, however. Members of the genus *Paphiopedilum* produce clumps of tufted growths. After flowering, these cease to grow themselves, producing instead one or more new side growths. In this way the whole plant gradually expands outward.

The second major growth pattern among orchids is the monopodial habit. Monopodial orchids do not expand indefinitely outward using a branching system of growths derived from a common base or rhizome. Instead, they produce a single, usually erect growth axis, a stem that grows continuously upward, branches rarely, and bears inflorescences only in its leaf axils. (In sympodial orchids the inflorescences may be basal, lateral, axillary, or terminal.) The stem bears roots at its base and adventitiously. Monopodial genera include the apparently stemless *Phalaenopsis* (see Plate 14) and the more typical *Vanda* and *Angraecum*.

The roots of terrestrial orchids more or less resemble those of other plants and are either long and string-like or thick, often covered with water-absorbent hairs. In epiphytic and lithophytic genera, the roots are different—generally thick, fleshy, and covered with a brittle spongy crust called velamen. This protective substance attracts and retains atmospheric humidity and fixes the roots to their anchor. Another feature of epiphytic orchid roots is that they contain chlorophyll. This is especially evident in their green growing tips. The presence of chlorophyll in the roots of epiphytic orchids has freed some genera from the need to produce green shoots and leaves altogether. The Asian *Chiloschista lunifera*, for

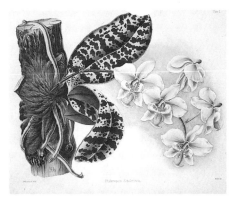

Phalaenopsis schilleriana, a monopodial orchid, from Warner, *Select Orchidaceous Plants*, plate 1

example, produces charming golden flowers from a leafless mass of ghostly gray roots.

Leaves

The foliage of orchids is no less variable than their flowers or growth habits. Orchid leaves can be deciduous or evergreen, thin textured and pliable, tough and rigid, or thick and fleshy. They range in shape from species to species, from the circular and broadly ovate to the narrowly linear. They may be flat, folded, or terete; puckered, veined, or warty; hairy or smooth. The only safe generalization one can make about orchid leaves is that many have a slight notch at their tips and a waxy, evaporation-saving coating on their upper surface.

For all this marvelous diversity, the leaves of orchids are not usually their prime attraction. In some genera, however, they are exceptionally beautiful. Several *Paphiopedilum* and *Phalaenopsis* species have foliage mottled with differing tones of green, gray, or even silvery white. Tropical cousins of two genera also found in temperate climates, *Liparis* and *Malaxis*, produce leaves that are richly stained with purple or bronze and patinated with metallic iridescence. The leaves of *Dactylorhiza* and *Orchis* can be handsomely spotted. A miniature denizen of South American cloud forests, *Lepanthes calodictyon*, produces shield-shaped, wavy-edged leaves on delicate stalks. Each blade is satiny emerald green netted with maroon. The Malaysian *Nephelaphyllum pulchrum*, pretty cloudleaf, has pale lime leaves flushed purple-red and finely veined with bronze. In the genus *Nervilia*, the leaves appear quite independently from the flowers. Large, heart shaped, and pleated, they resemble a stranded waterlily leaf or a stemless aroid and are often beautifully, if subtly, colored.

Phalaenopsis with characteristic fleshy and leathery leaves, from Warner and Williams, *The Orchid Album*, volume 2, plate 80

One group of orchids is famed for its foliage, however. The jewel orchids belong to the closely related genera *Anoectochilus, Ludisia* (syn. *Haemaria*), and *Macodes*. They hail from subtropical and tropical Asia and islands in the Indian and Pacific Oceans. Terrestrial and shade loving, these small evergreens have fleshy, creeping rhizomes, hairy roots, and narrow spikes of flowers that are usually described as insignificant. While it is certainly true that in most species the color range is limited to off-white, cream, green, and buff, in the most widely grown jewel orchid, *Ludisia discolor*, the flowers are sparkling white with a golden yellow column—a striking contrast to the dark foliage. The leaves of jewel orchids more than compensate for any disappointment caused by the flowers. Thinly fleshy and ovate to elliptic, they range in color from jade green to lime, blood red, maroon, chocolate brown, bronze, and black. The upper surface of each leaf appears silky or velvety, the result of thousands of minute, lens-like cells. More often than not, it is also exquisitely patterned with fine veins of glittering silver, gold, copper, or ruby red.

Mycorrhizal Symbiosis

Toward the end of the nineteenth century, a strange, enigmatic relationship between orchids and fungi was discovered that has yet to be fully explained. This phenomenon, known as mycorrhizal symbiosis (from *mycos*, fungus, and *rhizon*, root), is one of the most fascinating chapters in the entire field of orchid studies. It is not confined to orchids; many plant roots live in some type of symbiosis with fungi, exchanging nutrients. With orchids however, this relationship is essential to their survival.

The fungi concerned are microscopic organisms whose threadlike strands, hyphae, live inside the orchid root cells. The hyphae invade the surrounding terrain, breaking down organic matter and providing the plant with a ready supply of minerals and other nutrients. The plant in turn gives the symbiotic fungus sugars produced during photosynthesis.

The mycorrhizal relationships of orchids develop with the seed. Orchid seeds are minute and have scarcely any food reserves of their own. The fungal hyphae enter the embryo, stimulate it, and aid germination by providing nutrients. As the embryo develops, the hyphae become restricted to the roots. Mycorrhizal symbiosis becomes even more important when we realize that this is the only natural way for orchid seeds to germinate. In the past, this then unknown fact posed orchid growers their greatest difficulty: how to grow orchids from seed. At first, orchid seeds could be induced to germinate only by sowing them around the roots of their parents, and even then only sparsely and erratically. This mystery was explained away by mycorrhizal association. Once the symbiotic relationship had been discovered, seeds were sown in aseptic conditions in flasks containing agar jelly for support, porridge oats as fungal food, and a culture of the fungus concerned. Today the favored method is simply to sow seeds in sterile flasks on an agar substrate without the fungus but containing the mineral nutrients it would naturally have supplied.

Flowers

It is the flower that occupies the mind's eye when we speak of orchids. By far the plant's most conspicuous part, it holds us spellbound. Then again, no other plant family offers so seemingly infinite a variety of shape and color as do the thousands of orchid species. As extravagant, bizarre, and complex as they may appear, however, the basic structure of the orchid flower can be reduced to a simple equation with a recurring number three—an outer whorl of three sepals and an inner whorl of three petals. These are generally brightly colored and in a variety of shapes. In some genera, evolution has altered and simplified this pattern, reducing the number of sepals and petals by fusing them together.

One petal, called the lip or labellum, is clearly distinguishable from the others, differing in shape, size, and color, often larger and bulky, with brilliant colors and in strange shapes, patterned with spots, veins, hairs, and outlandish, often grotesque patterns. In almost all orchids, the labellum twists around 180 degrees when the flower blooms and is thus directed down and outward. This turns it into a landing platform for insect pollinators. From the flower center and projecting outward, almost parallel to the labellum, is the column, bearing the plant's sexual apparatus.

The column is a masterpiece of miniature, highly functional engineering. In other flowering plants the reproductive organs are separate. In orchids they are grouped together. The anther is located at the apex of the column—protected by a

Laelia tenebrosa, from Warner and Williams, *The Orchid Album*, volume 11, plate 487

detachable cap, the pollen is not powdery but bound together in two to eight sticky masses called pollinia. Just below the anther cap on the shaft of the column, we find the stigma, the receptive female organ. This consists of a small depression made receptive to the pollinia by a sticky liquid; the pollinia must come into contact with the stigma for fertilization to take place.

Fertilization

Nature's only reason for creating the flower, the justification for the existence of sepals and petals, the perfume they give out, and the amazing patterns traced on the labellum, is to enable fertilization. In the orchid family, fertilization is performed primarily by insects. Every orchid flower is a structure marvelously attuned to coerce one type of insect into removing the pollinia and carrying them over to the stigma of the next flower, completing the process of pollination. The relationship between plant and pollinator is both ideal and highly vulnerable, for its success can depend solely on a single insect species whose sudden disappearance would clearly be disastrous for the orchid's survival.

The genus *Cattleya* makes use of particular wasps and bees in Central and South America. In this case the insect, attracted by the showy flowers, alights on the labellum, which droops under its weight. This allows the insect to penetrate to the flower's center, drawn by the sweet perfume and its desire for nectar. Once the insect reaches the heart of the flower, the labellum—now free of the insect's weight—rises to resume its original position and traps the guest inside. Sooner or later the wasp or bee will try to leave. To do so, it is forced to wriggle around, hitting the pollinia, which stick to its back. Later, the insect will land on another *Cattleya* flower and repeat the process. In doing so the pollinia will be detached from the insect's back and become embedded in the stigmatic surface of the second flower, thus ensuring cross-fertilization.

Philip Reinagle, *Cupid Inspiring the Plants with Love*, from Thornton, *Temple of Flora*

The genus *Paphiopedilum*, with its bag-shaped, protruding lip, has a different pollination mechanism. Having fallen into this slippery, baffling sac, the insect finds that its only escape is to crawl through a tube-like structure formed by the in-rolled rear margins of the lip. The upper opening of this escape chute is partly blocked by a shield-shaped staminode. The pollen masses are delicately hinged to the staminode's base. The insect, if it is ever to escape, must brush past them, detaching the pol-

Cattleya brymeriana, from Warner and Williams, *The Orchid Album*, volume 4, plate 184

linia. These then adhere to the insect and are transported to another flower.

One orchid whose pollination mechanism was famously puzzling to naturalists past is *Angraecum sesquipedale* (Plate 1). This magnificent native of Madagascar has very large, waxy white, star-shaped flowers. Their nectar-bearing spurs can be more than a foot long (30 centimeters). Charles Darwin deduced that only an insect with a proboscis of the same length as the spur would be able to reach the nectar at its tip, and that some such insect—although then unknown to science—must exist somewhere in the forests of Madagascar and be pollinating the orchid. Darwin's hypothesis was met with some skepticism. Some went so far as to suggest that this orchid could have no insect pollinator, that the apparatus that had been thought to aid insect pollination (spur, nectar, fragrance) might not be after all, even that the species might not reproduce sexually. About forty years later, however, a moth was discovered in Madagascar with a proboscis of the correct length. In honor of Darwin's successful prediction it was named *Xanthopan morganii praedicta*.

Orchids belonging to the genus *Catasetum* have a very special technique that could be termed flinging. The flowers have a lip reminiscent of a cup or upside-down helmet, and a column very like a spring. Some insects are irresistibly attracted to the lip. As soon as they land they start sucking at it, activating highly sensitive hairs linked to the column. The column springs up, projecting the pollen masses onto the guest. The masses stick to its hairy body and are carried to the next flower.

Of all the many, varied tactics used by orchids for fertilization, one in particular arouses intense scientific interest even though it has not yet been fully explained.

Angraecum sesquipedale, from Warner, *Select Orchidaceous Plants*, plate 31

The role of the pollinator is played by euglossine bees from Central and South America. These bees are grouped into five different genera, some of which include dozens of species, some only one. Some species are found over a vast area, others only in a very limited locale. Some are large, others quite small. Almost all are brightly colored in shiny metallic hues of blue, green, and brown.

Laelia anceps var. *williamsii*, from Sander, *Reichenbachia*, volume 2, plate 3

Transverse section of ovary of *Bletia purpurea*, syn. *Bletia verecunda*, drawn by Franz Bauer in 1801, from Bauer and Lindley, *Illustrations of Orchidaceous Plants*, plate 9

Male euglossine bees are attracted by the flowers of certain orchids that offer no nectar. These orchids—*Anguloa* (Plate 2), *Stanhopea*, and other genera with massive, waxy blooms—do, however, exude an overwhelming perfume, vital in a tropical forest where dense vegetation occludes all senses but smell. The flowers' fragrance is found primarily in the lip in the form of microscopic liquid particles. It is produced and controlled by plant hormones that increase the scent according to the temperature and time of day and reduce it during bad weather or at night when insect pollinators are absent. Once fertilization has taken place the odor is no longer produced. Field studies have shown that all euglossine bees follow the same behavior pattern: they detect the orchid's perfume through their antennae, alight on the flower's lip, and move toward the area where the perfume is most intense, scraping the surface with the brushes on their front feet. They then wave their feet in the air, transferring the fragrant particles to their hind feet in the process; the entire operation is then repeated. The reason for the bees' behavior is still unclear even today. It is difficult to understand why the insects approach the flowers to collect the fragrant particles, but several hypotheses exist. The insects may need the essences to transform into elements needed for their own individual survival. Another real possibility is that the substances contain components that the bees use in turn to attract female bees.

Another great puzzle has to do with the couple of orchids that pass their entire life cycles underground. We have no idea whether they are fertilized with the help of organisms in the soil or whether they have mechanisms of self-fertilization. Self-pollination seems to be used by orchids as a rare, last-resort scenario. It occurs mainly in the absence of insect or other pollinators. The flower fails to open fully and the pollen masses lengthen until they come into contact with the stigmatic surface.

Insects perform the task assigned them extremely well. Pollen masses are normally carried on the insect's back although sometimes the head or proboscis is used. In some cases the pollinia move once they are on the insect's body. They rotate and lengthen to expose the side that sticks more easily to the stigma of the next flower. The pollinating agents found in Nature are missing from greenhouses or wherever orchids are cultivated, but pollination is still a relatively simple procedure. All that is needed is to remove the pollinia from beneath the anther cap at the end of the column and place them in the small sticky cavity just a few millimeters below.

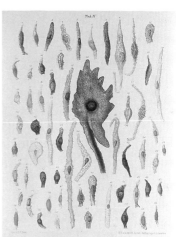

Orchid pods and seeds, from Beer, *Beiträge zur Morphologie und Biologie der Familie der Orchideen*

Once pollinated, the flower's task is over; with no further reason to exist, parts no longer needed are ruthlessly and immediately discarded. The flower that was previously open for weeks awaiting a pollinating agent fades away rapidly once its task is done, sometimes in only a couple of hours. Some days later a swelling can be seen at the apex of the column as the pollen masses are flattened more and more against the surface of the stigma and the ovary starts to enlarge. The pollen in the form of very fine tubes, aided by the sticky secretion in the stigma, start descending inside the column toward the ovary.

The ovary is circular in section and partitioned inside by three membranes that perform the same function as that of the placenta. Inside, the ovules develop slowly as the pollen tubes descend. Should this movement be interrupted, however, the entire mechanism is arrested. After sixty or more days, the pollen tubes have reached the ovary and deposit the sperm cells. These penetrate the ovules, which are now ready to receive them. Fertilization is thus complete. From this moment on, the activity of the embryo begins. It takes about six months for the ovary to grow, and about a year for the seed pod to ripen. At this point the fruit opens along three horizontal fissures and frees the seeds. The seeds are tiny and dust-like, consisting of a few embryo cells, a fine protective film, and almost no nutritional reserves. They are abundant, however. In some species more than three million seeds have been counted inside a single pod. Light as they are, they can travel for vast distances, carried by the slightest breath of wind. Only a few of them ever find suitable conditions for germination and develop into new plants. The remainder—sometimes millions—will scatter into oblivion.

Chapter 6

The Genera

To become even a little better acquainted with the vast world of the orchid family, we need to examine some of its main genera more closely. There are around twenty-five thousand species of orchids arranged in something like nine hundred genera. It would take a superhuman effort to account for them all. More realistically, we will look at some of the more commonly cultivated orchids to obtain some idea of their history, habitat, characteristics, appearance, and behavior—a sort of compass to help us orient ourselves.

Cattleya

Probably the most spectacular orchids of all are the members of the genus *Cattleya*. The flowers for the most part achieve a strangely harmonious union of billowing tepals and soft, glowing colors. These range from magenta to lilac, rose pink, and ruby red, from golden bronze to yellow, orange, and fiery vermilion, and from ocher to green and pure white. Often extravagantly large and heavily fringed, the labellum is suffused and veined with still more vivid and emphatic tones. Added to the shapeliness and brilliance of many *Cattleya* flowers is their perfume, which can fill a room.

There are some fifty *Cattleya* species found in Central and South America. Most are epiphytic although several species are lithophytes, growing on cliff faces, boulders, even rooftops. The pseudobulbs arise from a tough rhizome; this may be long and creeping, or short and congested, giving the plant a clumped appearance. The pseudobulbs themselves are slender and cane-like or more squat and club shaped. At their summits can be found one or two thick, leathery, evergreen leaves. The flowers emerge between the leaves in a short raceme protected at first by a tough sheath that may appear long before the buds themselves. The sepals are usually smaller and neater than the showy petals. The labellum is three-lobed, with the lateral lobes either outspread or in-rolled and forming a funnel, and the midlobe far larger and flamboyantly colored, often with a pattern of lines, tints, and veins to guide the insect pollinator toward the heart of the flower. The column, partly covered by the labellum, has four pollen masses at its apex.

Cattleya trianaei var. *backhouseana*, from Sander, *Reichenbachia*, volume 2, plate 1

This genus was named by John Lindley in honor of William Cattley (died 1832), a famous English orchid collector who successfully grew them as early as the beginning of the nineteenth century. He enthusiastically described *Cattleya* as "the most splendid, perhaps, of all Orchidaceous plants, which blossomed for the first time in Britain in the stove of my garden in Suffolk, during 1818, the plant having been sent to me by Mr. W[illiam] Swainson, during his visit to Brazil." The plant was the *Cattleya labiata*, the second member of this genus to reach Europe, having been discovered in the Organ Mountains of Brazil.

Astonishment like Cattley's at the sight

of this magnificent flower was to be repeated each time a new species reached the West. *Cattleya loddigesii* with lilac pink tepals and shell-like, cream, yellow, and rosy magenta lip had made its way to Europe from southern Brazil even earlier than *Cattleya labiata*. In 1826, fragrant, pale pink to purple-spotted *Cattleya intermedia* bloomed in the Glasgow Botanic Gardens. A tall plant with clusters of striking flowers (maroon-spotted, olive to lime green tepals and a white and ruby to garnet lip) reached London from Rio de Janeiro in 1827. This was *Cattleya guttata*. Then, in Guatemala during the 1830s, George Ure Skinner discovered *Cattleya aurantiaca* with dense clusters of small, starry, orange-red flowers. In 1836 he discovered *Cattleya skinneri*, named in his honor. *Cattleya mossiae* with languorously spreading, deeply ruffled, lilac pink petals reached Europe from Venezuela in 1836. In 1839, *Cattleya walkeriana* was discovered in Bahia, Brazil. Far smaller than *Cattleya mossiae*, its exquisitely scented flowers are neatly shaped and range in color from pinkish lilac to magenta with a deep amethyst or purple-red lip. The same year also brought the discovery of the Brazilian *Cattleya aclandiae*, a small plant with large flowers whose tepals are ocher blotched with maroon in somber contrast to the lip, which is white, heavily stained with rosy purple. In 1840, Europe saw the arrival of *Cattleya granulosa*. This tall species bears clusters of heavily scented green flowers with a white lip patterned in orange-yellow and crimson. Then, in 1848 or 1849, Józef Ritter von Rawicz Warscewicz discovered *Cattleya warscewiczii* in Colombia. The fragrant flowers of this species can be as much as 8 inches across (20 centimeters), with dusky pink tepals and a velvety carmine lip marked with two golden white blotches. In the mid-nineteenth century the same plant hunter discovered *Cattleya dowiana* in Costa Rica. This large-flowered species is remarkable in having bright golden tepals and a contrasting, ruby red lip, valuable colors used extensively since in orchid hybridization. *Cattleya dowiana* was soon lost, however, only to be rediscovered a decade later when it was named in honor of Captain Dow whose ship transported dozens of orchids and orchid hunters.

So it could be said that most of the important *Cattleya* species were discovered and introduced in the first half of the nineteenth century. Since then, the list of species has lengthened considerably. On their arrival in European horticulture, cattleyas excited such vociferous enthusiasm that they became the classic prototype of "the orchid" in the public imagination.

Cymbidium

The name *Cymbidium* is derived from the Greek *kymbe*, boat, a reference to the base of the lip, which resembles the hull of a ship. This genus is one of the most important for orchid growers, and certainly the most widely grown and extensively bred. It consists of about fifty species found principally in India and China, where they have been admired and grown for thousands of years, but also east to Japan and south to Indonesia and Australia. The large-flowered modern hybrids tend to be Himalayan in ancestry, descended from species native to the green Khasi Hills, the valleys of Tibet, and the slopes of the Himalayas at elevations up to 6,600 feet (2,000 meters).

Cymbidium lowianum, from Warner and Williams, *The Orchid Album*, volume 10, plate 471

These orchids are mostly terrestrial with exposed ovoid pseudobulbs sheathed by leaf bases and growing slowly outward in a clump. The evergreen leaves are usually long, slender, arching, and pliable but can be rigid and succulent (*Cymbidium aloifolium*) or erect and paddle shaped (*Cymbidium devonianum*). The cooler growing, Chinese and Japanese species are almost grass-like in overall appearance. The flower spikes emerge from the base of the pseudobulb enveloped with sheathing bracts. In some species, the spikes bear only one or two flowers, but most of the cultivated species and hybrids bear many flowers in erect to arching racemes.

The beauty of *Cymbidium* is more subdued than that of *Cattleya* and derives from the overall effect of the long, flower-covered racemes. The spreading petals and sepals are basically oblong to lanceolate in shape and similar in size and form. The lateral lobes of the lip stand erect or curve inward like an open tube or, more appropriately perhaps, a boat. The midlobe is larger and curves downward like a tongue; it is usually patterned with lines, veins, or spots and is sometimes hairy. The flowers are rather waxy and have an exceptionally long life—from six weeks to three months. Many of the cultivated species and hybrids are large, to 5 feet tall (1.5 meters), although several of those hailing from China and Japan are dwarf and have been used in breeding programs to create miniature hybrids ideal for the home, conservatory, and smaller greenhouse.

Here are just a few of the more important species. One of the first known in the West was *Cymbidium aloifolium*, native to a vast area covering India, Indochina, and Indonesia. Hendrik Adrian van Rheede tot Draakestein had originally described it, under a different name, in his *Hortus Indicus Malabaricus* (1678–1703). It is a rather charming plant with small flowers borne in pendulous racemes. The tepals are cream, striped and stained with blood red or deep chestnut, as is the lip except for the bright yellow callus. Southeast Asia is home to *Cymbidium finlaysonianum*, introduced to the West at the beginning of the nineteenth century. This is a large epiphyte with pendulous racemes to more than a yard or meter long. Scented in the morning, the small flowers have olive green tepals stained wine red, and a white lip, marked red at the base, with a yellow callus. One of the most exquisite species lives in Myanmar, the former Burma, and northeastern India. *Cymbidium tigrinum* is a small, broadly leaved plant with proportionately large, fragrant flowers. The tepals are ocher, the uppermost sepal arching inward with the petals and the lower sepals spreading outward. The lip is brilliant white spotted and barred with purple-red or rusty brown.

It lives as a lithophyte in Nature and prefers elevations up to 8,200 feet (2,500 meters). The intrepid orchid hunter, Reverend Charles Samuel Pollock Parish, discovered it in the mountains of Tenasserim, Burma, in 1863.

The range of *Cymbidium devonianum* extends from the slopes of the Himalayas to Sikkim and then from Assam to Thailand. Plant hunter John Gibson discovered it in northeastern India in 1837 when scouting the area for orchids for the duke of Devonshire, after whom it is named. It is a small, broadly leaved species with strongly pendulous racemes of small, fleshy flowers, the tepals bronze-green combed with purple-red and the lip a rich maroon. *Cymbidium iridioides* (syn. *Cymbidium giganteum*) extends from the Himalayas into Indochina. It was discovered by Nathaniel Wallich in 1821 and has large, fragrant flowers, the tepals olive green striped maroon and the lip yellow spotted bloodred. This species is part of the genetic makeup of many modern hybrids to whom it has bequeathed its yellowish green hue.

Finally, there are the Australian species. Unlike many of their cooler growing Asian counterparts, the following species do better in intermediate to warm conditions. *Cymbidium canaliculatum* was described by Robert Brown in the *Prodromus Florae Novae Hollandiae* in 1810. This epiphyte grows in the hollows of trees. It produces strongly keeled, rigid leaves and arching, densely flowered racemes. The flowers are as much as 1⅝ inches across (4 centimeters) and vary greatly in color, the tepals ranging from olive to bronze streaked with red-brown or solid, dark maroon, and the lip ivory spotted, lined or edged purple or red. Introduced into European cultivation in 1840, the epiphytic *Cymbidium madidum* resembles *Cymbidium canaliculatum* in habit. It, too, produces long and arching racemes crowded with small, waxy, scented flowers. Yellow with chestnut exteriors, the tepals point forward; the lip is primrose, striped with gold and blotched red-brown.

Dendrobium

The Greek words *dendron*, tree, and *bios*, life—an allusion to the epiphytic behavior of many of these orchids—combine in the name of this diverse genus of more than one thousand species. *Dendrobium* has an immense distribution, from India to New Zealand, including much of Asia and all of Oceania. To describe the orchids in general terms is a difficult matter, such is the sheer variety of a genus so large and evolving in so wide a range of climates and habitats.

Dendrobium contains evergreen and deciduous species. In many, the pseudobulbs resemble clumped, fleshy canes with the flowers and leaves at their nodes or summits. Others, like *Dendrobium bellatulum*, are smaller with squatter pseudobulbs. Some of the species native to New Guinea are truly miniature, with bead-like pseudobulbs and outsized flowers of luminous beauty. The Australian *Dendrobium cucumerinum* lacks pseudobulbs altogether, merely consisting of a creeping network of succulent, gherkin-shaped leaves.

In size, shape, and color, the flowers of *Dendrobium* vary correspondingly. The basic outline consists of four more or less similar tepals and a rounded, shallowly funnel-shaped lip. Flowers may be solitary, clustered, or carried in racemes. Few other orchid genera exhibit colors so vivid as some species of *Dendrobium*. These range from white to rose, fluorescent pink, purple, red, and orange to yellow, green and cream, with the center of the labellum sporting hues and markings almost too brilliant to be true.

One interesting Asian species is *Dendrobium albosanguineum*, discovered by Thomas Lobb growing along the Attram River, near Moulmein in Burma. It has perfumed, cream blossoms with tinges of yellow. The labellum and column take on a purplish tone. *Dendrobium bellatulum* is from an area a little farther north. It was discovered by Augustine Henry at Mengzi in the Chinese province of Yunnan where this epiphyte lives at elevations up to 5,200 feet (1,600 meters). It has fragrant flowers with snow white tepals and petals and a bright yellow labellum stained orange-red to salmon pink. In the same area of montane forest in Myanmar, Laos, and Thailand lives *Dendrobium brymerianum* (Plate 5), named in honor of the British member of Parliament who first managed to induce it to flower in cultivation. Its flowers are magnificent: tepals shining yellow, the lip stained orange at its center, and with deeply cut, lace-like edges.

Dendrobium densiflorum extends from the slopes of Nepal to Thailand. Its pendulous racemes carry a multitude of fragrant flowers. These are golden yellow with a velvety orange, fringed lip. *Dendrobium nobile* comes from more or less the same area. This familiar and popular orchid has large flowers in shades of white, pink, and rosy purple; the lip is usually paler at the margin, with a dark purple-red blotch in the throat. Australia and New Guinea are home to *Dendrobium discolor.* Originally collected by Joseph Banks along the Endeavour River during Captain Cook's journey to Australia, this robust species produces swarms of yellow-brown flowers with twisted and ruffled tepals. Also Australian, *Dendrobium kingianum* is a compact plant with dense sprays of neat and fragrant flowers in shades of white, pink, and magenta. From the Solomon Islands, New Ireland, and Vanuatu, the former New Hebrides, comes *Dendrobium gouldii* with slender, upwardly spiraling petals that range in color from pure white to yellow. Finally, there is the remarkable *Dendrobium lasianthera*, a species growing to more than 6½ feet tall (2 meters) with long sprays of large flowers. The tepals are a deep, glossy bronze suffused with purple-red and edged in gold; the lip and column are deep magenta, highlighted by a golden anther cap. Although first described in 1932, this species was lost and then rediscovered in

Dendrobium densiflorum, from Warner and Williams, *The Orchid Album*, volume 7, plate 303

New Guinea during the Second World War by Captain Blood, who returned to its swampy, crocodile-infested habitat to collect new specimens once the war was over.

Epidendrum and *Encyclia*

Although epiphytic orchids were being grown in continental Europe as early as the 1730s, the first epiphytic species to bloom in British horticulture was probably *Encyclia cochleata* (syn. *Epidendrum cochleatum*), which flowered at Kew in 1787. This species produces long-lasting spikes of flowers with pale green, ribbon-like tepals. These hang downward but the lip is held aloft. Creamy white with dark purple markings, the lip resembles a small shell, hence this species' popular names, cockle or clamshell orchid. Until more recently, the two genera *Encyclia* and *Epidendrum* were combined in *Epidendrum*, and it is still not uncommon to find what are properly *Encyclia* species named as *Epidendrum*. In very general terms, *Epidendrum* species tend to have clumps of cane-like stems whereas *Encyclia* species tend to be pseudobulbous. Both are large genera, totaling more than 650 species between them and populating an area that includes Florida, the Caribbean, Central America, and northern South America.

These orchids are closely allied to *Cattleya*. Indeed, one of the best known species of *Encyclia*, *Encyclia citrina*, with gray-green foliage and large lemon yellow flowers, was once classified as *Cattleya citrina*. As a rule, however, the flowers are far smaller than those of *Cattleya* and produced in greater abundance, either in long racemes and panicles or clustered in the middle of the plant

Epidendrum erubescens, from Bateman, *The Orchidaceae of Mexico and Guatemala*, plate 32

as if they had been carefully placed there by some invisible hand. Although small, the flowers often have such lively, bright, and cheerful colors that they stand out vividly against the green backdrop of foliage. The genus *Encyclia* includes some of the most heavily scented orchids, among them the *Encyclia fragrans* with its intoxicating odor and the deliciously perfumed *Encyclia alata* (syn. *Epidendrum alatum*), a native of Central America. In the genus *Epidendrum*, the ghostly white and yellow-green flowers of *Epidendrum nocturnum* emit their sweet perfume only at night.

Examples of more flamboyant *Encyclia* species include the large-flowered *Encyclia cordigera* (syn. *Epidendrum atropurpureum*), with wavy chestnut tepals and a spreading, deep rose lip, *Encyclia prismatocarpa* (syn. *Epidendrum prismatocarpum*), with large and fragrant yellow-green flowers spotted and barred with brown or black, and *Encyclia vitellina*, with gray foliage and spikes of flowers in brilliant scarlet or cinnabar red. Outstanding *Epidendrum* species include *Epidendrum ibaguense* (syn. *Epidendrum radicans*), tall and reedy with an everlasting succession of small, cross-like flowers in shades of red, orange, and pink, *Epidendrum pseudepidendrum*, apple green flowers with a glossy, crimson to orange lip, and *Epidendrum stamfordianum*, with dainty flowers massed in pendulous racemes, the tepals yellow-green marked maroon, the lip white patterned magenta at its base and olive marked maroon at the tip.

Laelia

Named after one of the Vestal virgins, *Laelia* (Plate 8) is an important genus for orchid growers. Its seventy or so species live on trees and rocks in Central and South America. In their tough, fleshy leaves and the shape of the rhizome and pseudobulbs they closely resemble *Cattleya*. Their flowers, too, are *Cattleya*-like but have eight pollen masses rather than four. *Laelia* flowers tend to be smaller but what they lack in size, they easily make up in the intensity of their coloring. *Laelia* species hybridize readily with *Cattleya*, producing crosses to which they transmit bright, vibrant tones.

One species well deserving mention is *Laelia albida*. Its small, scented flowers are pure white or rose tinted; the underside of the column is covered with tiny crimson dots and the lip is stained bright yellow at its center. *Laelia albida* comes from Mexico, especially the western side of the cordiliera where it grows usually on old oak trees. It was first introduced in 1832 by Baron Wilhelm Friedrich Karwinski, who found it near Oaxaca.

Another species from the same area of Mexico, often to be found in orchid collections, is *Laelia anceps*, with large flowers borne on curved stalks. The petals and sepals are a delicate mauve-pink and the lip is edged with dark purple-red and marked with showy red streaks in the golden throat. *Laelia cinnabarina* is decidedly lithophytic in habit, growing as it does on the rocks of Brazil at elevations up to 4,900 feet (1,500 meters). The pseudobulbs and leaves are long and slender, as is the inflorescence, which grows to 28 inches long (70 centimeters) and bears as many as fifteen orange-red, exquisitely shaped flowers. Introduced into European gardens in 1836, it lends itself very well to cross-breeding and its warm and glowing tones can be seen in numerous hybrids. One of the most celebrated species is *Laelia jongheana*, also native to Brazil where it grows in humid mountain areas. It was discovered in 1856 by Joseph Libon, who sent it to Belgium. The flowers are large and pink to amethyst purple and the wavy lip is white-tipped with a bright yellow center.

The genus also includes some miniature orchids such as *Laelia lundii*, a native of Brazil where it was discovered in 1880 by Eugenius Warming. The flowers are no larger than an inch across (2.5 centi-

Laelia anceps var. *scottiana*, from Warner and Williams, *The Orchid Album*, volume 7, plate 325

meters) and predominantly pure white; the lip, however, is marked with rosy purple veins that lead into the flower's center, where they dissolve into solid magenta.

Among the larger species, *Laelia perrinii* is another lovely Brazilian native that has been known since the first half of the nineteenth century. Its flowers closely resemble a *Cattleya* and can be 6 inches across (15 centimeters). The tepals are mauve-pink and the lip is a rich purple-red with a yellow-white blotch in the throat. *Laelia purpurata* is even larger with white or pink, *Cattleya*-like flowers to 8 inches across (20 centimeters); the lip is deeply edged and veined with magenta or violet. The local name in Guatemala for *Laelia rubescens* is flor de Jesús. This species bears large sprays of scented flowers, ranging in color from pure white to palest rose or lilac with a dark maroon blotch in the throat. Native also to Costa Rica, Nicaragua, and Mexico, it was introduced to Europe in the first half of the nineteenth century.

Miltonia and *Miltoniopsis*

Recognizing *Miltonia* and *Miltoniopsis* is easy. The petals and sepals are rounded and open, and the lip is broad and spreading, giving the flower a flattened shape very similar to a pansy. Sometimes delicately scented, the flowers are carried in arching racemes and are between 1¼ and 3 inches across (3–7 centimeters). Comprising about twenty-five species in all, these two genera were formerly united in *Miltonia*, a genus named by John Lindley for Lord Fitzwilliam Milton (1786–1857), an English patron of botany and an enthusiastic orchid grower. More recently, the "Andean miltonias," six species found in wet cloud forest from Costa Rica to Peru, have been moved to the genus *Miltoniopsis*. The remaining, true miltonias are mostly from Brazil, with one species found in Peru. Miltonias have enjoyed somewhat fluctuating fortunes in horticulture. Toward the end of the nineteenth century they were immensely popular. Many hybrids were produced and these found favor especially as gentlemen's boutonnieres.

The Brazilian native *Miltonia clowesii* was discovered in the 1830s by George Gardner in the Organ Mountains near Rio de Janeiro. The flowers have narrow, pointed tepals wonderfully banded orange and dark red-brown, in sharp contrast to the purple-blotched, bright white, and fan-shaped lip. Although less showy, *Miltonia flavescens* also deserves mention. Its fragrant flowers are pale yellow and star shaped with a wavy labellum covered with crimson spots. It was discovered by Michel Étienne Descourtilz in Brazil, in the state of Minas Gerais, during the first half of the nineteenth century. *Miltonia regnellii*, from the same area, was discovered in 1846 and was brought to Hamburg in 1855. Rounded and open, the flowers are white, delicately tinged with pale pink, lilac, or lavender-mauve, a coloration that deepens toward the center of the lip. Then, there is *Miltonia spectabilis*, which has the honor of being the first member of the genus to reach Europe, arriving in 1850 probably from eastern Brazil. It is an impressive plant, producing up to fifty blossoms at a time, each on its own stalk. The typical plant has yellow-white tepals tinted red toward their base, and a large, broad lip suffused and veined with purple-red. More common in cultivation, however, is variety *moreliana* with rich plum purple tepals and a dark rose, strongly veined lip.

Miltonia spectabilis var. *moreliana*, from Warner and Williams, *The Orchid Album*, volume 8, plate 364

Miltoniopsis warscewiczii (syn. *Miltonia endresii*) was discovered in 1849 by Józef Ritter von Rawicz Warscewicz in the Costa Rican cordillera. It is a small plant with long, thin leaves. The perfumed flowers are broad and rounded. They are white, shaded pale mauve pink, and yellow at the center. A similar species is *Miltoniopsis phalaenopsis* (syn. *Miltonia pha-*

laenopsis), originating in Colombia where it grows in humid, shady regions at elevations up to 4,900 feet (1,500 meters). Louis Joseph Schlim discovered it on the western slopes of the Andes in 1850. The plant has grassy, light green leaves set against which are ample, open flowers, milky white marked with a magenta or purplish crimson and yellow in the center. The most common species in private collections is *Miltoniopsis vexillaria* (syn. *Miltonia vexillaria*) from Colombia and Ecuador. This species has broad, flat, white flowers stained yellow at the center and suffused or overlaid with pink, mauve, or even dark red. Although it was first discovered in 1866 by a plant hunter working for the English nursery Messrs. Veitch, these specimens never reached British shores. It was later rediscovered first by Gustav Wallis and then by Benedikt Roezl, who brought it to Europe in 1872.

The last plant in this group, *Miltonia warscewiczii*, is now more properly known as *Oncidium fuscatum* or *Miltonioides warscewiczii*. Discovered in 1830 in the Peruvian Andes by the German botanist Eduard Friedrich Poeppig, this unusual species bears large sprays of sweetly perfumed flowers. The tepals are small, wavy, and rusty brown with a white or yellow margin. The lip is far larger and white overlaid with purple-red and with a central zone of glossy red-brown. In name if not in looks, this species can be easily confused with *Miltoniopsis warscewiczii*.

Odontoglossum

The three hundred species of *Odontoglossum* (Plate 10) broadly defined, live on the Pacific side of the Andean slopes at elevations between 4,900 and 16,100 feet (1,500–4,000 meters). The name derives from Greek *odous, odontos*, tooth, and *glossa*, tongue, referring to tooth-like processes found on the lip. Like many of the older and larger orchid genera, *Odontoglossum* has more recently been split into a number of smaller groupings (*Cuitlauzina, Lemboglossum, Osmo-*

glossum, Otoglossum, Rossioglossum), leaving some sixty species of true odontoglossums. In this work, these species are still treated as *Odontoglossum* with the new name given after the old. Predominantly epiphytic, the members of this genus have ovoid or rather flattened pseudobulbs and strap-shaped leaves. The flowers are carried like a flight of butterflies in racemes or panicles that may be up to a yard or meter long. They are close to those of *Miltonia* but more varied in size and shape. Sometimes they recall brightly colored stars; at other times they are wavy or curly, as if ruffled by the wind, or trace delicate, airy patterns like mid-winter frost on a window pane. One of the most graceful species is *Odontoglossum cirrhosum* with large, snow white flowers, the tepals narrow, lacy, and sometimes spotted red-brown, the lip bright gold. In contrast, *Odontoglossum grande* or *Rossioglossum grande* earns its common names of tiger or clown orchid by having bold golden flowers that are barred with chestnut brown and sport a callus which resembles a comic figure.

Odontoglossums need bright but indirect light, abundant humidity, and cool, buoyant atmosphere to thrive—a combination that is quite normal in their homeland but difficult to re-create elsewhere. This does not mean that growing them is impossible, and many of the modern hybrids resemble the species but are easier to grow.

Sadly, we have room to mention only a few of the dozens of odontoglossums that deserve discussion. The first to reach Europe was *Odontoglossum bictoniense* or *Lemboglossum bictoniense*, discovered by George Ure Skinner in Guatemala in 1835. The plant grows at elevations of more than 9,800 feet (3,000 meters). The flower stalks are erect, narrow, and to a yard or meter tall. To 2 inches across (5 centimeters), the fragrant flowers have olive green tepals blotched

Odontoglossum grande or *Rossioglossum grande*, from Warner and Williams, *The Orchid Album*, volume 2, plate 79

with red-brown, and a white and magenta lip. *Odontoglossum cordatum* or *Lemboglossum cordatum* also hails from Central America. Its narrow yellow-brown flowers are dark spotted and striped, resembling a spider or some other strange animal that stalks the tropical forest.

We must not forget *Odontoglossum crispum*, which some consider unquestionably the most beautiful orchid in existence. It was first discovered by Karl Theodor Hartweg in 1841 in the Colombian Andes where it thrives at an elevation of 9,800 feet (3,000 meters). Arching gracefully, the racemes are often a yard or meter long. Resembling white lace, the flowers are broad, crystalline in texture, and finely toothed or fringed. The lip is stained yellow, often with a few random red spots. Native to the high-altitude forests of Colombia and Venezuela, the fragrant *Odontoglossum odoratum* was first collected by Jean Linden in 1842. Its flowers have narrowly pointed and wavy, yellow tepals liberally blotched with chocolate brown.

Finally, there is *Odontoglossum rossii* or *Lemboglossum rossii*. This orchid comes from Mexico and other Central American areas where it grows in humid forests. It was discovered by J. Ross in 1837 in Oaxaca. The large, wavy flowers are a splendid glowing white, striped with red-bronze.

Oncidium

A cascade of living confetti, or golden rays of sun scattered by a crystal prism—this gives a vague idea of the beauty of the genus *Oncidium* (Plate 11). This highly varied genus comprises some 450 species of epiphytes and lithophytes living in the American tropics and subtropics. It takes its name from Greek *onkos*, fleshy body, an allusion to the warty callus of the flower. In size, these orchids range from true dwarfs, the whole plant only a few centimeters across, to giants with much branched, scrambling inflorescences decked with hundreds of flowers. In habit they may be pseudobulbous or consist merely of leaves. Plants of the second type include small species with flattened fans of foliage (these sometimes included in the genera *Psygmorchis* and *Tolumnia*) and the "mule's ear" oncidiums, plants such as *Oncidium cavendishianum*, with very reduced or absent pseudobulbs and a single large, fleshy leaf. The long flower stalks tend to bear large, sparse flowers or branch into a multitude of tiny, delicate flowers that sway with every breath of wind. Usually slight and brightly colored, the tepals encircle a large lip, giving birth to fantastic creatures that our imaginations may perceive as lithe ballerinas, strange animals, and sparkling jewels.

Oncidium was the genus that sparked the orchidmania that swept through Europe at the beginning of the nineteenth century. The very existence of this genus alone, with its wealth of species, would be enough to give orchids a special place in creation, so great is their variety. Each species offers unique details of color and shape, bound to escape one at the first dazzling sight of the flowers.

Just to mention a few of the multitude of superb species—*Oncidium ampliatum* was discovered in Costa Rica by Hugh Cuming in 1831. It thrives in the hot, humid areas found at low elevations. Numerous pale yellow blossoms with red-brown spots hang in bunches along flower stalks to more than a yard or meter tall. As is so typical of this genus, the flowers call to mind brightly clad human figures. Another lovely species is *Oncidium crispum*, brought to Europe from Brazil around 1832. The large tepals are chestnut brown with yellow to buff spots and streaks along their crisped and wavy edges. Ruffled and pleated, the semicircular lip is yellow with a brown-mottled margin. Brown is also the dominant color of *Oncidium falcipetalum*. Its flowers are very human in outline, with outspread, arm-like petals, longer, leg-like lateral sepals, and the

Oncidium splendidum, from Sander, *Reichenbachia*, volume 2, plate 2

small fleshy lip constituting the torso. All parts are wavy and glossy chocolate brown, variably blotched, spotted, or outlined in bright yellow. This remarkable species lives in an area that includes Venezuela, Colombia, Ecuador, and Peru, usually in montane forests.

Brazil is the homeland of *Oncidium marshallianum*, discovered by H. Blunt in the Organ Mountains in the state of Rio de Janeiro. Its flowers are wide open, wavy, and crinkled. They are yellow and red-brown, and again, of a bizarre, definitely humanoid shape. *Oncidium kramerianum* or *Psychopsis krameriana* is one of the most famous orchids. Borne one at a time in long succession, the extraordinary flowers resemble giant butterflies, with the narrow dorsal sepal and petals pointing, antennae-like, toward the sky. The wing-like lateral sepals curve downward, golden yellow mottled red-brown and with tightly crisped margins. Large, rounded, and frilled, the lip is yellow with fox red margins. Another much celebrated species, *Oncidium papilio* or *Psychopsis papilio*, is closely related to *Oncidium kramerianum* or *Psychopsis krameriana*, differing only in its larger flowers, clearer in color and carried on longitudinally flattened stalks. It was brought to England in 1826 by Sir Ralph Woodford, the governor of Trinidad. The excitement stirred by its first appearance marked the advent of orchidmania.

Paphiopedilum and Other Slipper Orchids

The slipper orchids belong to a different subfamily of orchids altogether, the Cypripedioideae. They are characterized by having their lateral sepals usually fused in a single organ called the synsepalum. Over this lies the lip, shaped like a pouch or slipper and holding within its aperture a shield-like staminode that covers the pollinia. The petals and dorsal sepal are usually similar in color and spread away from the lip. The flowers are borne on terminal spikes, singly or in racemes. Most species are terrestrial and all lack pseudobulbs.

Of the four or five genera of slipper orchids, *Cypripedium*, a genus of about thirty-five herbaceous perennials, has the most widespread distribution: North and Central America, Europe, and Asia. *Paphiopedilum*, the popular Venus's slipper orchid with some seventy species and innumerable hybrids, is found in tropical and subtropical Asia, the Philippines, the Malay Archipelago, and the Solomon Islands. *Phragmipedium* (Plate 15) resembles *Paphiopedilum* in its evergreen tufts of two-ranked, strap-like leaves. It comes from Central and South America, however, and several of the species have spectacularly long, ribbon-like petals. Members of *Phragmipedium* were once included in *Selenipedium* a genus now confined to five extraordinary tropical American slipper orchids with reed-like growth to 16½ feet tall (5 meters). To confuse matters further, all the above genera have in the past been classified under *Cypripedium*.

In structure, the long-lasting flowers of *Paphiopedilum* may well be among the most surprising to be found throughout the many genera of Orchidaceae. The lip juts forward, looking like a sac or a sabot shoe, one of Nature's most outrageous yet perfectly designed inventions. In many species of *Paphiopedilum* the flowers are rather rigid and glossy, covered with a smooth layer of wax. The colors are often darker than in many other orchids—greens, purples, blacks, browns, dull yellows, blood reds, and dusky pinks—and there is usually a pattern of lines, veins, streaks, and dots laid out to encourage pollination. There may also be dark hairs, fringing the petals or springing from mole-like warts. On the whole, the flower looks like some alien, anomalous creature, seeming to transcend the vegetable world and at times emanating an indefinably sinister air. It looks for all the world like a visitor from an unknown planet. Yet for many, *Paphiopedilum*

Paphiopedilum venustum, from Warner, *Select Orchidaceous Plants*, second series, plate 24

is synonymous with "orchid" and numerous growers have dedicated all their efforts to raising them.

Phalaenopsis

The genus *Phalaenopsis* takes its name from Greek *phalaina*, moth, and *opsis*, appearance. About fifty species of moth orchids can be found from tropical Asia south to the Australasian tropics. They are especially abundant in the Philippines. They are monopodial epiphytes with very short stems and neither rhizomes nor pseudobulbs. For this reason they store reserves of moisture in their leaves, having drawn it with their large, ample roots, which hang over the void in forests or wrap themselves around the nearest prop.

Broad and large, each plant's few leaves are thick with a leathery surface. The upper side is deep green or beautifully patterned with silver, and the lower surface often tinged red. The flowers are carried on racemes that emerge from the base of the plant or the older leaf axils. These may be as much as 13 feet in length (4 meters). In many species, and especially in hybrids, the inflorescence will branch with age and may continue to produce flowers for several seasons.

Phalaenopsis speciosa, from Warner and Williams, *The Orchid Album*, volume 4, plate 158

The *Phalaenopsis* hybrids and species we most frequently encounter have large flowers with rounded sepals and petals. The most common hybrids are white or pink, with a small, anchor-shaped lip suffused yellow and dotted red. The lip can also be the same basic color as the petals, only in a more intense shade, or a color in complete contrast with the rest of the flower. The flowers may open in succession or all together, each lasting as much as four months. Some hybrids will bloom more than once a year. There are, of course, species with very different flowers, some tiny and quite beautiful—it is a great shame that even today these are still largely exiled to the greenhouses of specialist growers.

It is difficult to find the right words to describe the effect of a *Phalaenopsis* in flower. The blooms, neatly arranged along the stalk, are all turned in one direction as if they were observing the admirer. In contrast to the few, simple, and low-lying leaves, the elegant flower stalk appears to be suspended in the air. Few orchids can compete with this genus for delicacy and grace. And they repay the care they receive with great generosity of bloom, a fact that has encouraged many novice orchid growers to begin their endeavors with *Phalaenopsis*.

One species that deserves particular mention is *Phalaenopsis amabilis*, found from the Philippines to Queensland, Australia. It was one of the first exotic orchids known in the West. Rumphius described it at the end of the seventeenth century. Carl Ludwig Blume chose it as the basis of the new genus *Phalaenopsis*, which he named in 1825. The plant has a few leathery leaves and the curved stalk bears a number of large white flowers with a contrasting yellow labellum, spotted with red. It is one of the most commonly cultivated orchids.

Phalaenopsis equestris comes from the Philippines and Taiwan. Its flowers are tinged with pink, and the purple labellum is yellow in the center with red lines and dots. The Philippine Archipelago is also home to *Phalaenopsis lueddemanniana*, a variable species with white or rose flowers heavily patterned with concentric rings of mauve-pink. After pollination, the flowers turn green—very rare among these orchids, as is their fragrance. *Phalaenopsis schilleriana* (Plate 14) is yet another Philippine native. It bears branched sprays decked with dozens of large, pale pink flowers, their lips stained yellow and dotted with red. In addition to its surpassingly lovely blooms, this species has ornamental foliage, dark green intricately mottled with silver. Again from the Philippines, *Phalaenopsis stuartiana* resembles the *Phalaenopsis schilleriana* in its free-flowering habit, flower shape, and beautifully colored leaves. The flowers are white with a yellow-stained lip spotted with dark red. It grows on the island of Mindanao where it was discovered by William Boxall in 1881. Finally, we have *Phalaenopsis violacea* from the Malay Peninsula and Borneo. This species grows in damp, shady areas near riverbeds. Although somewhat dwarfed by the leaves, the small, short-stalked flowers are very beautiful—fragrant and rich magenta, or greenish white stained with violet.

Vanda

Vanda derives its name from the Sanskrit name *vanda*, originally used in Bengal for *Vanda tessellata*. The genus comprises some fifty species found throughout eastern Asia from the Himalayas to the Malay Peninsula. They have vastly different cultural requirements, depending on where they grow. Some grow on cool mountain peaks in the Himalayas and Indochina. Others descend to the Malay Peninsula, spreading out over the Pacific equatorial zone. They may be epiphytic or lithophytic. Most, however, love exposure to the sun's rays. Some vandas have now been placed in the segregate genera *Esmeralda*, *Euanthe*, *Holcoglossum*, *Papilionanthe*, *Trudelia*, and *Vandopsis*, but the genus is treated here in its traditional sense.

Vandas are widely admired, and justly so. They are monopodial like *Phalaenopsis* but develop a stem that, with its continuous growth, can reach a length of 8¼

Vanda cathcartii or *Esmeralda cathcartii* from Warner and Williams, *The Orchid Album*, volume 4, plate 168

feet (2.5 meters). Cylindrical or strap shaped, the leaves sit opposite each other along the stem so that at a distance the plant resembles a small palm or reed. Long, thick roots sprout from the base of the stem but can also develop among the leaves, either embracing the branches of trees or hanging over empty space—all of which gives *Vanda* an unexpected air, a feeling of faraway places and great beauty, even without its flowers.

The flowers are carried, sometimes in their dozens, on racemes that sprout from the leaf axils on the younger part of the plant. The lip is not especially showy; it is the sepals and petals, flat and round, that are large and full of color. This coloring can be quite remarkable. Blue, for example, is a rare color indeed among orchids, but famously to be found in *Vanda coerulea* (Plate 16). This species was discovered by William Griffith in 1837 in the hills of Assam, where it was growing on old oak trees at elevations of more than 3,300 feet (1,000 meters). This coveted species has been crossed with the Philippine *Vanda sanderiana* or *Euanthe sanderiana*, which bears large, rosy green flowers heavily tessellated with rusty brown. The resulting grex, *Vanda* Rothschildiana, produces magnificent, flat blooms in pale lilac checkered with lavender blue. Another well-known species is *Vanda teres* or *Papilionanthe teres*, discovered at Sylhet in what is now Bangladesh by Nathaniel Wallich in 1829. Its native range extends from Thailand to the Himalayas, usually in warm valleys where this species grows on large trees. It has terete leaves and large, wavy flowers, beautifully colored in tones of soft pink, gold, and mauve. *Vanda* or *Papilionanthe* 'Miss Joaquim', a cross between this species and the closely related *Vanda hookeriana* or *Papilionanthe hookeriana*, is the national flower of Singapore, and many other terete-leaved *Vanda* hybrids have since been developed for the cut flower trade. Another popular species is *Vanda tricolor* (syn. *Vanda suavis*), originally from Java where it was discovered by Thomas Lobb in 1846. Firm and waxy white, its tepals are heavily patterned with red-brown in vivid contrast to the magenta or purple lip.

European Orchids

Europe is also populated with orchids, albeit sometimes rather sparsely. In some areas, however, native European orchids are so successful that they have colonized roadside verges and suburban lawns. There are even records of some species' having stolen into cities, haunting churchyards and loitering in quiet parks. Few people realize they are there, yet wild-orchid enthusiasts spend boundless energy in their pursuit. Immune to the blandishments of more exotic genera, they spend days on end combing field, fen, and forest to observe, study, and admire their native species.

The European orchids are certainly quite unlike their flamboyant foreign cousins. They are so much smaller that they often escape notice, as if they were invisible, camouflaged inhabitants of the fields. But to make their acquaintance is well worth our while, opening as it does one of the most interesting chapters in the world of Nature—unfamiliar for all that it is in our midst, and rich in surprises.

Orchids grow in abundance all through Europe, from the Mediterranean as far north as Scandinavia. Wild orchids are particularly plentiful in Italy, with its favorable geographic position and varied terrain. One hundred or so species of European orchids divide into about thirty genera, found in a wide range of habitats from coastline to alpine peak, bog to chalk grassland, scrub to dense forest. Changing land use, agricultural chemicals, deforestation, and the depredations of collectors have all contributed to their plight—in some cases close to extinction.

The European species are terrestrial and herbaceous. Some are rhizomatous, many tuberous. Their leaves are grassy, strap shaped, oval, sword-like, or lacking altogether in the four saprophytic genera. Most flower in spring and summer. The root systems of two of the best known genera, *Orchis* and *Ophrys*, consist of two rounded tubers, no larger than 2 inches across (5 centimeters). At first glance they unequivocally recall the male genitalia, a resemblance noted in ancient times. Not all genera have such testicular tubers, however.

They can also assume other, always peculiar shapes—the fingers of *Dactylorhiza*, for example, which has given rise to a variety of legends. The tubers' main function is to act as a reservoir for water and nutrients. The plant uses one of them, larger and plumper, during the present growing season, the other having been used the season before.

Ophrys

The genus *Ophrys* comprises thirty species found in Europe and the Middle East. They have always attracted the interest of botanists because of their remarkable mimicry of pollinating insects. Denizens of grasslands, woodland fringes, rocky slopes, and heath, they are small plants with sparse flowers that can easily pass unobserved. The tepals are small and delicate, pink, white, or green, sometimes marked with maroon. The thick, ample lip is rich brown, maroon, or yellow. At the center of the lip is a distinctively shaped zone. Shiny and metallic, this zone, the speculum, ranges in color from bright blue to violet and is bordered with lines and patterns. The broad apex of the lip is velvety, and in many species the margins of the lip are fringed with dense, dark hairs. In color, shape, texture, and sometimes even odor, the whole ensemble creates the perfect likeness of a wasp, bee, or hornet.

It is not only the human eye that is deceived by this likeness. Lacking nectar to attract pollinators, *Ophrys* species use another expedi-

Ophrys holoserica, syn. *Ophrys fuciflora*, from Schulze, *Die Orchidaceen*

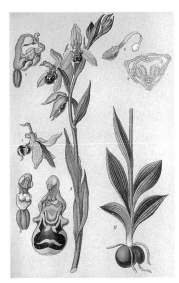

Ophrys apifera, from Schulze, *Die Orchidaceen*

ent, disguising themselves to look like female insects. When a male wasp, bee, or hornet sees an *Ophrys* flower as it dances through the wild grass, it heads for the lip, mistaking it for a female of its own species. The insect tries to copulate but all its efforts are futile since the false female, obviously, is not exactly responsive. The more the insect tries to excite some reaction, the more it pushes against the pollen masses, which then stick to its back. Finally tiring of its frigid mate, the frustrated insect flies away. A few yards or meters away, it spies another flower of the same species of *Ophrys* and alights, mistaking it for another female and manifesting the same behavior. In this way the pollen of the first flower brushes against the stigma of the second. Before leaving, the insect may pick up the pollen masses of this flower in turn and carry them to a third, thus performing the vital work of cross-pollination quite inadvertently. In some cases this system has evolved with remarkable efficiency, for the males of the pollinator species emerge before the females and are able to find only the flowers of their orchid deceivers.

Most lovingly described by Darwin, these reproductive rites have attracted the interest not only of botanists but also of commentators anxious to deny the possibility of such fantastically devious systems. Some imaginative moralists have read debauchery into the insects' behavior, while others prefer to see the insect as a satyr dedicated to endless games of love in secret country places.

Flowers of the genus *Orchis*, from Tournefort, *Elemens de Botanique*

Orchis

The genus *Orchis* comprises some thirty-five species found predominantly in Europe and the Mediterranean. As noted, *Orchis* takes its name from the Greek word for testicle, which the tubers of this genus closely resemble. During the first warm days of spring, when the countryside is at last verdant once more, colonies of brightly colored *Orchis* can sometimes be spotted in woodlands and meadows, often near streams. Sword or strap shaped, the leaves are sometimes spotted with purple. They sheathe an erect stalk 6–40 inches tall (15–100 centimeters) in whose upper reaches the flowers can be found arranged in a raceme. The tepals curve forward, hooding a showy lip. The many bizarre guises that the lip can assume are reflected in such common names as bug orchid, military orchid, butterfly orchid, lady orchid, and monkey orchid.

The colors are clear, delicate, and lively, darkening from pink to purple and from white to yellow with lines and dots in more intense tones of the same color. The spur, a tiny tube containing nectar for insect pollinators, protrudes from the back of the lip. The effect of these plants when in flower is one of striking beauty, often enhanced by a subtle perfume.

Orchis militaris, from Schulze, *Die Orchidaceen*

Cypripedium calceolus

Cypripedium calceolus is the only species of the genus found wild in Europe. It is also the most celebrated European orchid, though it is also native to Asia and North America. Its common name is yellow lady's slipper. Popular imagination associates this flower with mountain elves, envisioning mysterious spirits enclosed by the golden labellum—bizarre hypotheses sparked by its peculiar appearance.

The plant is rhizomatous with a few broad and ribbed leaves along an erect stem. The

Cypripedium calceolus, from Schulze, *Die Orchidaceen*

stem terminates in a nodding stalk, usually bearing a solitary flower. The tepals are a lovely reddish brown or purple, the petals narrow and turning in an elegant spiral. Appearing strangely inflated, the slipper-shaped labellum is luminous golden yellow. When an insect falls into this sac, its only escape is a pair of narrow openings to the rear. These force the pollinator to brush past the pollinia, which then stick to its body and are carried to the next flower. Sadly, this exquisite species, with its delicate apricot scent, has paid a dear price for its beauty and is seriously threatened with extinction. This fate also threatens its magnificent North American cousins. These include the glorious white and rose *Cypripedium reginae*, the subtle, chocolate and dusky pink *Cypripedium acaule*, and the neat, multiflowered, white and green *Cypripedium californicum*.

Epipactis palustris, from Schulze, *Die Orchidaceen*

Epipactis

Epipactis, from the ancient Greek name for these plants, is a genus of some twenty-four species. *Epipactis* is found as far afield as tropical Africa, Asia, and Mexico but the best known species are native to cool temperate regions of Europe and North America, where they grow in grasslands, woodland fringes, damp dunes, and along streamsides. They are rhizomatous plants with leafy stems terminating in racemes of nodding flowers. The flowers are often turned in only one direction whereas the sepals and petals jut forward, encircling a large labellum with wavy, serrated

Serapias hirsuta, from Schulze, *Die Orchidaceen*

edges. Inside the lip is a cavity filled with nectar for insect visitors. The column rises over the labellum, offering up the ample pollen masses. Flower color varies according to the species, from orange to yellow to brown, rosy pink to white, and violet to purple, highlighted by the yellow-tipped column and giving rise to contrasting and subtle but very harmonious tones.

One of the most familiar European species is *Epipactis palustris*, the marsh helleborine, damp loving and with purple and olive tepals and a white lip traced with pink and yellow. In the North American *Epipactis gigantea*, the flowers have orange-yellow tepals stained with bronze and a yellow-white lip combed with purple-red. This species is very vigorous, soon forming large clumps in the garden.

Serapias

Serapias is another remarkable genus of European orchids. It takes its name from Serapis, the ancient Egyptian bull deity, and its ten or so species are found predominantly in the Mediterranean but also as far north as Brittany, Switzerland, and even southern England. They prefer warm, sunny areas and are seen in meadows, sandy dunes, and damp areas along the coast.

They have rounded tubers and sword-shaped leaves. The flower spikes may grow to 20 inches tall (50 centimeters). The flowers themselves are rather subdued, if not sinister, in coloring, and bizarre in structure—from a helmet-like hood of tepals protrudes a large labellum. Differently colored, hairy, glistening, or heavily veined, the labellum points down, earning these plants their common name, tongue orchid.

PLATE I
Angraecum sesquipedale
Warner and Williams, *The Orchid Album*, volume 11, plate 518

PLATE 2
Anguloa hohenlohii
Warner and Williams, *The Orchid Album*, volume 1, plate 19

PLATE 3
Brassia arcuigera
Warner and Williams, *The Orchid Album*, volume 4, plate 159

PLATE 4
Cattleya dowiana var. *aurea*
Warner and Williams, *The Orchid Album*, volume 2, plate 84

PLATE 5
Dendrobium brymerianum
Warner and Williams, *The Orchid Album*, volume 9, plate 398

PLATE 6
Dracula roezlii
Warner and Williams, *The Orchid Album*, volume 5, plate 243

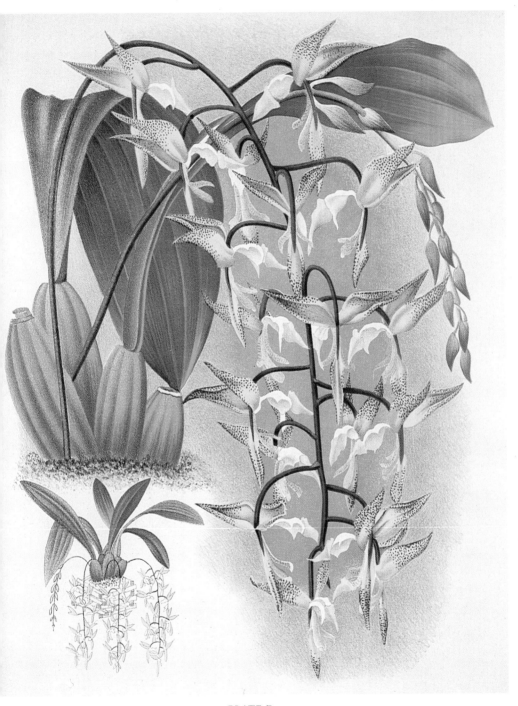

PLATE 8
Laelia elegans
Warner and Williams, *The Orchid Album*, volume 9, plate 413

PLATE 9
Masdevallia coccinea 'Atrosanguinea'
Warner and Williams, *The Orchid Album*, volume 3, plate 105

PLATE 10
Odontoglossum ×*eugenes* (*O. nobile* × *O. spectatissimum*)
Warner and Williams, *The Orchid Album*, volume 3, plate 355

PLATE 11
Oncidium lamelligerum
Warner and Williams, *The Orchid Album*, volume 7, plate 315

PLATE 12
Paphinia grandiflora
Warner and Williams, *The Orchid Album*, volume 4, plate 145

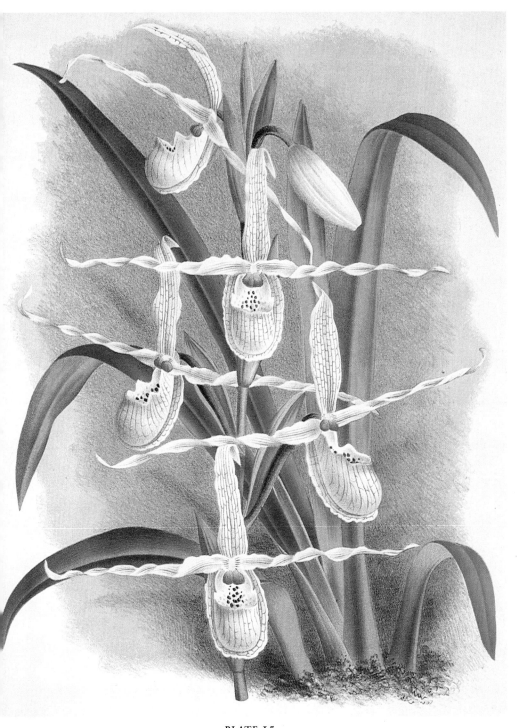

PLATE 15
Phragmipedium reticulatum
J. Linden, *Lindenia*, volume 1, plate 10

PLATE 16
Vanda coerulea
Warner and Williams, *The Orchid Album*, volume 11, plate 517

Chapter 7

Growing Orchids

To grow an orchid is to gain mastery over a piece of Nature. It entails selecting, from all the possible species available, those that most arouse our curiosity and inveigle us into the mystery of their exquisite beauty. Easy to maintain, the overwhelming lavishness of modern orchid hybrids might initially attract our interest. Or we might succumb to the more elusive charms of the species, which evoke faraway lands and are usually more difficult to grow than the hybrids. This seemingly endless abundance of kinds of orchids combined with the kaleidoscopic diversity they represent are what drives people to collect them.

The process of seduction and initiation in the culture of orchids has, after all this time, developed firm rules and first rites. The scene is a horticultural classic, the script well tested, indeed repeated again and again over the nineteenth and twentieth centuries and likely to be played out as long as there are orchids and orchid lovers. The first plant, bought or received as a gift, piques our curiosity. A sense of euphoria leads us to pore over this exotic, alien object suddenly so close at hand. We admire its strange flowers, astonishing colors, the texture of the petals, the succulent leaves, and the fleshy roots that crawl out of the pot. We generously care for and nurture the plant but the extraordinary flowers slowly fade. The withered orchid is placed alongside the other houseplants, all hope of seeing it bloom again gone.

Then, quite unexpectedly, a few months later, something happens and a new shoot begins its irritatingly slow growth. We closely follow this development as it lengthens and proves to be no mere leafy growth but a new and budding inflorescence. Overjoyed, we ask ourselves whether this small miracle was due to special care or sheer luck. Whichever the reason, this success goads us into buying a second and then a third plant—after all, they are not nearly as expensive as we thought. We talk with other, more established orchid owners and press them for part of some magnificent specimen that, we argue, must be sorely in need of division. We start buying books on orchids. The newcomers colonize windowsills and the more favored corners of the house. Before we know it, we are hooked, orchid lovers without realizing it.

Growing orchids is actually far from difficult. Making them flower regularly may be a little harder, but by way of recompense it is almost impossible to kill them. The basic rules are few and essentially similar to those for growing most other plants. The most important thing is to have some understanding of the orchid's natural

Growing orchids, from de Puydt, *Les Orchidées*

habitat. This kind of knowledge provides information—ideal climate; light, water, temperature, and humidity requirements; clues as to suitable potting media and growing regimes—all of which are vital if the life that the orchid enjoys in Nature is to be reproduced in cultivation.

There is no real need for a greenhouse, even a small one. With just a few elementary steps, many orchids will thrive and flower on windowsills. The amateur orchid grower needs to combine the basic rules of gardening with intuition and a little information—and be willing to attempt new growing methods. With some skill and a sprinkling of good luck, simple solutions will be found to complex problems.

Potting Media

Since they differ from other plants in so many respects, one would perhaps expect orchids to have highly distinctive needs in terms of potting media. Epiphytic orchids live suspended over the void, their roots anchored to the branches of trees and exposed to the open air. Much of their water requirement is met by atmospheric humidity and by rainfall either falling directly onto the plant or percolating through the canopy. The roots of such orchids are spongy, absorbent, and adapted to exposure—it would be disastrous to bury them in a compacted potting medium whether soil based or soilless.

The needs of many tropical and subtropical terrestrial species are similar to those of epiphytic species. Members of the genera *Cymbidium* and *Paphiopedilum*, for example, have fleshy, clinging roots adapted to life among exposed tree roots or rocks, or within a loose layer of leaf litter.

Orchids growing on the windowsill, from L. Linden, *Les Orchidées Exotiques*

Cooler growing terrestrials like *Cypripedium* and *Orchis* need a finer, denser substrate, but these too are highly intolerant of poorly drained or stagnant soils. To generalize, a successful orchid substrate must have certain properties: it must decompose very slowly, permit a great deal of internal aeration, and allow free drainage.

Formerly, the most popular potting medium for orchids was osmunda fiber. This open, versatile medium consisted quite simply of the dark, wiry roots of *Osmunda regalis*. This magnificent fern, however, was so heavily overcollected in the past that it is now threatened in the wild and protected by law from the depredations of orchid growers. Another group of ferns, the tropical and subtropical tree ferns, still provides fiber for the grower, demand supposedly not having endangered supply. Tree fern fiber is denser and far more rigid than osmunda. It is usually purchased in hard, dark, fibrous blocks that can be broken down into an excellent coarse potting medium or used as they come for mounting epiphytic orchids. Sometimes tree fern fiber blocks are sold compacted and hollowed, making ideal hanging pots for epiphytes.

Two other potting media whose exploitation is a far from happy thing are moss peat and its progenitor, sphagnum moss. Used in coarse, compressed lumps, moss peat is excellent for many epiphytes, cymbidiums, and some paphiopedilums. In the looser, finer state in which it is usually bought, moss peat needs to be mixed with polystyrene granules, vermiculite, charcoal, or live *Sphagnum*. With some adjustment, this mixture can be made to suit almost all orchids, from robust, tropical epiphytes like *Cattleya* and *Dendrobium* to hardy herbaceous terrestrials such as *Bletilla*, *Cypripedium*, and *Dactylorhiza*. Generally speaking, the thicker rooted, more succulent, and more obviously epiphytic the species, the higher the proportion of aerating additives to peat should be. Picked free of weeds, debris, and pests, live sphagnum moss is a valuable ameliorator of orchid potting mixes, retaining water and promoting root development without causing stagnation. It is especially useful with very young plants and the finer rooted species. Sphagnum moss is also used to line baskets and as cushions for epiphytic orchids mounted on branches, wooden rafts, and slabs of bark and tree fern. However, using moss peat is hardly good conservation practice. Whenever possible, substitute with coir, composted bark, or leaf mold. Rock wool is a good substitute for sphagnum moss.

Without doubt, the most widely used orchid growing medium is sterilized, dry conifer bark. This substance is inert, slow to decompose, and very freely draining. Orchid bark is offered in various grades. The finest bark, that is, the one with the smallest particles, suits dwarf, or wiry or fibrous rooted species; young plants; species with high or continuous moisture requirements; and herbaceous terrestrial orchids. Coarse bark is appropriate for robust plants with well-developed pseudobulbs, thick roots, and tough or succulent leaves. In either case, perlag, perlite, polystyrene, charcoal, and perhaps sphagnum moss may be added to varying degrees.

Several other potting media are used for orchids. Materials usually added to mixes include coir, fibrous peat, leaf mold, loam, coarse grit, and silver sand—all especially valuable for hardy terrestrial species. One material seen with growing frequency is water-repellent rock wool, used either pure or mixed with perlite. As a wholly nutrient-free medium that easily becomes too wet or too dry, rock wool should be used only within a carefully calculated regime of watering and feeding. That said, this material encourages rapid and extensive rooting and, for commercial growers at least, has produced astonishing results across a very wide range of subtropical and tropical orchids.

With a family so diverse as Orchidaceae, it is nearly impossible to make safe generalizations about potting composts, which tend to vary from plant to plant, from grower to grower, and from situation to situation. It would, for example, be foolish to attempt a *Cymbidium* in very coarse bark (a medium that ideally suits it) if that plant were to be grown in the fierce dry heat of the house. Conversely, planted in a dense, water-retentive medium, that same *Cymbidium* might soon perish if grown in a wet and humid greenhouse.

Pots

Orchids can be grown in a wide variety of containers. Terra-cotta pots undoubtedly provide the most attractive and healthy homes for the majority of orchids. Three flaws are sometimes attributed to clay pots: that orchid roots cling to their interiors and are damaged during repotting, that the clay itself accumulates toxic deposits from hard water and fertilizers, and that clay pots dry out too quickly. These are mostly nonsense. A healthy orchid will produce abundant roots. Should some be broken during repotting, the plant is unlikely to be harmed. Orchids are usually repotted too frequently to allow a dangerous level of salt deposits to build up in the pot. When watering, however, ensure that water flushes right though the compost. Also, wash clay pots thoroughly before using them. The most common problems in orchid cultivation are overwatering and poor soil aeration—clay pots breathe, often a great advantage. Clay pots are, however, expensive, fragile, do dry out quickly, and are difficult to handle and regulate en masse. Plastic pots have none of these drawbacks and are especially suited to very open, bark- or perlite-based media.

Orchids in a pot, from Burbidge, *Die Orchideen*

Pot for epiphytic orchids, from Burbidge, *Die Orchideen*

Clay or plastic, any successful orchid container must have excellent drainage. This usually takes the form of one or two holes at the bottom of the pot in which case it may be necessary to enhance the drainage with a layer of rocks, pebbles, or clay aggregate granules. Purpose-made orchid pots of the late nineteenth and early twentieth centuries were perforated throughout with large holes, allowing the passage of air and water and the rambling of aerial roots. These find their modern equivalent in plastic pots that are effectively loosely meshed baskets.

Containers for epiphytic orchids become increasingly open, to the extent that they can barely be said to be containers at all, more crude approximations to the plants' treetop habitats. Epiphytic orchids grow well, for example, in hanging baskets made of plastic, wire, or classically, slatted wood. Genera such as *Dracula* (Plate 6), *Gongora* (Plate 7), and *Stanhopea*, with pendulous flower spikes, will grow in little else. Still more open is the raft, a suspended raft-like grid of slatted wood to which the plant is wired against a cushion of moss. Epiphytes can be also grown mounted on blocks of tree fern fiber, cork, or bark, or tied to the branches of trees. Orchids grown in this way will require high humidity and frequent misting or plunging, at least when in growth.

Light

Orchids are very sensitive to light: they love it, they seek it, they need it. We need to look at the way orchids grow in Nature to grasp how much light they need. In their natural habitat, epiphytic and lithophytic orchids thrive on trees and rocks—some growing in full exposure, others lower down where they can receive some degree of shade. This wide range of light preferences can also be found in terrestrial orchids, some of which grow in open meadows, marshes, and mountainsides, whereas others can be found in the darkest recesses of the forest. For all that, it can safely be said that few orchids will tolerate full summer sunlight in cultivation. Those that will

A window transformed into a greenhouse, from L. Linden, *Les Orchidées Exotiques*

tend to be thick-leaved epiphytic genera such as *Cattleya*, *Laelia*, and fleshy-leaved *Oncidium*, and even these will scorch, their leaves becoming spotted and discolored. Genera such as *Anguloa* (Plate 2), *Calanthe*, *Lycaste*, and *Phaius*, for example, with broad, soft leaves, suffer terribly if grown in direct sun. Orchids such as *Ludisia*, *Paphiopedilum*, and *Phalaenopsis* have a marked preference for shade.

Most genera will fail to produce healthy pseudobulbs and fully developed flowers unless they receive full sunlight in the dark winter months, and light shade between mid-spring and mid-autumn. Windowsills, where orchids are frequently grown, like greenhouses become veritable ovens if exposed to direct sunlight without a breath of wind. Plants left there are soon found with dried-out, spotted leaves, the sign of irreparable burns. Some screening, a blind, or whitewash, to block the full force of the sun's rays, becomes essential. A bright windowsill treated in this fashion can house dozens of genera, from *Vanda* to *Cattleya*, *Cymbidium*, *Odontoglossum*, and *Oncidium*. More shady windows can host splendid specimens of *Phalaenopsis* and *Paphiopedilum*. Experience is still the best guide to turning every corner of your home into a tropical microcosm.

Temperature

Since orchids grow in such a wide range of climates and habitats, a few species at least can usually be found to fit whatever conditions the would-be orchid grower can offer. Many modern hybrids are far more tolerant than their parents and forbears: well-chosen grexes and clones of *Cymbidium*, *Dendrobium* (*bigibbum* and *nobile* types), *Miltonia, Miltoniopsis, Odontoglossum, Oncidium, Paphiopedilum, Phalaenopsis,* and ×*Vuylstekeara* can be used as houseplants with minimal fuss.

Subtropical and tropical orchids are divided into three temperature bands for ease of cultivation. Cooler growing orchids need a minimum winter night temperature of 45°F (7°C). In summer, the nighttime minimum can hover around 55°F (13°C). Cooler growing genera include *Cymbidium, Coelogyne* (some), *Dendrobium* (some), *Disa, Dracula* (Plate 6), *Masdevallia* (Plate 9), *Miltonia, Miltoniopsis, Odontoglossum* and hybrids, *Paphiopedilum* (some), and a wide range of other species usually from high altitudes. Intermediate growing orchids need a minimum winter night temperature of 58°F (15°C). They include such genera as *Aerangis, Brassavola, Brassia* (Plate 3), *Bulbophyllum, Cattleya, Dendrobium* (some), *Encyclia, Oncidium* (some), *Laelia, Paphiopedilum* (some), *Vanda* (some), and many others. Warmer growing orchids need a minimum night temperature of 68°F (20°C). Among this group are the larger *Angraecum* species, *Catasetum* and allies, *Dendrobium* (some), *Paphiopedilum* (some), *Phalaenopsis, Psychopsis* (some), *Vanda* and many of its allies and hybrids, and foliage orchids like *Anoectochilus* and *Macodes.* These three temperature categories are not hard and fast. Some orchids will adapt to all three environments. Some intermediates will grow happily in the cool collection, others in the warm, and most cool and warm orchids will survive—perhaps even thrive—in the intermediate collection. When growing orchids in the home, such distinctions tend to become academic in any case, but they are offered here as guidelines.

Of course, temperatures will rise in summer. It is not, however, advisable to let any orchid become too hot, that is, hotter than 88°F (31°C). The effects of overheating can be mitigated by ventilation, shading, frequent damping down, and syringing. For cooler and intermediate growing orchids, summer temperatures should drop at night. Where this cannot be achieved under glass or in the house, move more robust plants, large cymbidiums, for example, outdoors for the summer to a sheltered, shaded spot.

In climates that experience little or no frost, some genera may well spend winter outside too. Cymbidiums adapt effortlessly, and a number of orchid enthusiasts are attempting to do the same with *Oncidium* and *Odontoglossum*. This tendency to nudge exotic plants once commonly thought delicate into the great outdoors is to be encouraged because it can lead to some serendipitous surprises. If a certain English gardener had never left exposed to the rigors of winter *Camellia* plants that later bloomed magnificently, who knows how long we would have cosseted them in greenhouses?

Fully hardy orchids include *Cypripedium* (European and North American species), *Dactylorhiza*, *Epipactis*, and *Orchis*. These grow readily in the open garden. Although hardy, genera such as *Calypso*, *Ophrys*, and *Serapias* prefer the sheltered, controlled conditions of the alpine or cold greenhouse, as do several terrestrial genera from Australia, most notably *Corybas* and *Pterostylis*. Orchids from cool temperate East Asia—*Bletilla*, *Calanthe*, *Cypripedium*, and *Pleione*— thrive in the unheated greenhouse, but may also survive year-round outdoors in sheltered places and if protected in winter with a mulch, cold frame, or horticultural fleece.

Moisture

Re-creating the humid atmosphere of the tropics inside our houses is a difficult undertaking and not one with which other family members will always sympathize. For the home orchid grower, dry heat given off by central heating poses a real threat to these humidity-loving plants. The simplest remedy for this problem is to keep the plants away from radiators and other direct sources of heat and to stand them on dishes or trays containing a layer of moist gravel. Evaporation from the gravel protects the plants in an envelope of humidity. The pots themselves should never stand in water, as saturation leads quickly to root death and rots.

It is estimated that about eighty percent of all plants that die in houses do so from drowning. The percentage is even higher with orchids because of the cherished but erroneous notion that abundant watering ensures good health. There is no overall rule as to how often orchids should be watered since their needs vary according to the genus and species. But there are certain common themes. No orchid thrives when constantly wet. With the exception of some terrestrial species, few even prosper when constantly moist. It is usually preferable to allow the potting medium to dry briefly between thorough, drenching waterings. This is true if the plant is actively growing. If, however, the orchid is one that requires a distinct dry period when not in growth, then watering of any sort other than the lightest spray may be a disaster. Orchids that need a dry rest tend to have thick, leathery, evergreen or sometimes deciduous leaves and stout pseudobulbs. They are for the most part epiphytes and lithophytes. When their roots and shoots are growing, be generous with water, humidity, and food. When growth stops—but not during flowering, which may occur when a plant is at rest—keep the plant drier and cooler.

Orchids that grow continuously such as *Paphiopedilum* and *Phalaenopsis* can be watered and fed more or less year-round. Orchids grown in pots should be watered heavily—until water runs freely from the drainage holes. Again, do not water them unless they need it, which may be more seldom than one would imagine. Orchids grown in baskets or mounted on bark, branches, and rafts should be plunged or sprayed regularly when in growth. All orchids appreciate syringing, but take care to avoid allowing water to rest in any growth likely to rot, or on leaves that may scorch.

Light, temperature, and humidity are the three main factors that determine our plants' destiny. Plants work at full

Orchid placed on a saucer containing water for extra humidity, from L. Linden, *Les Orchidées Exotiques*

rhythm on sunny days and thus need more nourishment and water. Conversely, they function at a minimum on dull, dark winter days. An orchid lover will swiftly learn that his or her plants thrive when their environment and culture are in harmony—nature with nurture, grower and plant both reaping the rewards of attention.

Sources

The following books were consulted for information and, as indicated in the captions, as sources of illustrations for the present book.

Allan, M. 1967. *The Hookers of Kew, 1785–1911*. London.

Avicenna (Ibn Sīnā). 1608. *Canon Medicinae . . . .* Venice.

Barrettand, H., and J. Phillips. 1987. *Suburban Style*. London.

Bateman, J. 1837–1843. *The Orchidaceae of Mexico and Guatemala*.

Bateman, J. 1867. *A Second Century of Orchidaceous Plants*. London.

Bauer, Francis, and J. Lindley. 1830–1838. *Illustrations of Orchidaceous Plants*. London.

Bechtel, H., P. Cribb, and E. Launert. 1992. *The Manual of Cultivated Orchid Species*, third edition. London and Cambridge, Massachusetts.

Beer, J. G. 1863. *Beiträge zur Morphologie und Biologie der Familie der Orchideen*. Vienna.

Bishop, G. 1990. *Travels in Imperial China, the Explorations and Discoveries of Père David*. London.

Bishop, I. L. 1900. *Chinese Pictures, Notes on Photographs Made in China*. London.

Black, P. M. 1973. *Orchids*. London and New York.

Blunt, W. 1971. *The Complete Naturalist, a Life of Linnaeus*. London and New York.

Burbidge, F. W. 1875. *Die Orchideen der Temperirten und Kalten Hausen.* Stuttgart.

Burbidge, F. W. 1880. *Gardens of the Sun . . . A Naturalist's Journal on the Mountains and in the Forests and Swamps of Borneo and the Sula Archipelago.* London.

Carter, H. B. 1988. *Sir Joseph Banks, 1743–1820.* London.

Chancellor, J. 1973. *Charles Darwin.* London.

Chieh Tzu Yuan Hua Chuan. 1679–1701. *The Mustard Seed Garden Manual of Painting.* Shanghai edition, 1887–1888.

Claire, R. 1998. *David Douglas (1799–1834), Naturaliste Écossais, Explorateur de l'Ouest Américain.* Drulingen, France.

Coats, A. M. 1969. *The Quest for Plants, a History of Horticultural Explorers.* London.

Curtis, S. 1820. *The Beauties of Flora . . . .* London.

da Costa, Cristovao (Christobal Acosta). 1585. *Trattato . . . .* Venice.

Dalechamps, J. 1586–1587. *Historia Generalis Plantarum . . . .* Lyon.

Darwin, C. 1862. *On the Various Contrivances by Which British and Foreign Orchids Are Fertilised by Insects . . . .* London.

Darwin, E. 1789. *The Botanic Garden; a Poem, in Two Parts.* Part 2, *The Loves of the Plants.* London. Translation into Italian by G. Gherardini: 1805. *Gli Amori delle Piante.* Milan.

de L'Écluse, C. (Carolus Clusius). 1601. *Rariorum Plantarum Historia . . . .* Antwerp.

Della Porta, G. B. 1588. *Phytognomonica.* Naples.

de Puydt, E. P. 1880. *Les Orchidées . . . .* Paris.

Desmond, A. J., and J. B. Moore. 1991. *Darwin.* London.

Desmond, R. 1992. *The European Discovery of the Indian Flora.* Oxford.

Desmond, R. 1995. *Kew, the History of the Royal Botanic Gardens.* London.

Desmond, R. 1999. *Sir Joseph Dalton Hooker, Traveller and Plant Collector.* Woodbridge, Suffolk, England.

Dioscorides Pedanius. *De Materia Medica.* Frankfurt edition, 1543.

Dodoens (Dodonaeus), J. R. 1569. *Florum, et Coronariarum Odoratarumque Nonnullarum Herbarium Historia . . . .* Antwerp.

Dufour, P. S. 1685. *Traitez Nouveaux & Curieux du Café, du Thé et du Chocolate . . . .* Lyon.

Dupree, A. H. 1959. *Asa Gray, 1810–1888.* Cambridge, Massachusetts.

Ferrari, G. B. 1633. *De Florum Cultura . . . .* Rome.

Fortune, R. 1847. *Three Years Wandering in the Northern Provinces of China . . . .* London.

Fuchs, L. 1542. *De Historia Stirpium Commentarii Insignes*. Basel.

Griffiths, M., and J. Stewart. 1995. *Manual of Orchids*. London, and Timber Press, Portland, Oregon.

Gunn, M., and L. E. W. Codd. 1981. *Botanical Exploration of Southern Africa*. Cape Town.

Hadfield, M., R. Harling, and L. Highton. 1980. *British Gardeners, a Biographical Dictionary*. London.

Holder, C. F. 1892. *Charles Darwin*. London and New York.

Hooker, J. D. 1854. *Himalayan Journals*. London.

Hooker, W. J. 1851. *A Century of Orchidaceous Plants . . . .* London.

Jameson, A. 1900. *Sacred and Legendary Art*. London.

Jellicoe, G., S. Jellicoe, P. Goode, and M. Lancaster. 1986. *The Oxford Companion to Gardens*. Oxford and New York.

Kaempfer, E. 1712. *Amoenitatum Exoticarum*. Lemgo, Germany.

Kerner von Marilaun, A. 1887–1891. *Pflanzenleben*. Leipzig. Translation into Italian: 1892. *La Vita delle Piante*. Turin. Translation into English: 1894–1895. *Natural History of Plants*. London.

Lees-Milne, J. 1991. *The Bachelor Duke, a Life of William Spencer Cavendish*. London.

Lemmon, K. 1968. *The Golden Age of Plant Hunters*. London.

Lewis, M. W. H. 1990. Power and Passion: the Orchid in Literature, pages 207–249 *in* J. Arditti (editor), *Orchid Biology, Reviews and Perspectives*, volume 5. Timber Press, Portland, Oregon.

Linden, J. 1885–1906. *Lindenia, Iconographie des Orchidées*. Ghent.

Linden, L. 1894. *Les Orchidées Exotiques*. Brussels.

Lindley, J. 1837–1841. *Sertum Orchidaceum . . . .* London.

Lindley, J., and J. Paxton. 1850–1853. *Paxton's Flower Garden*. London.

Lyte, C. 1983. *The Plant Hunters*. London.

Massingham, B. 1982. *A Century of Gardeners*. London.

Mattioli, P. A. 1554. *Commentarii . . . de Materia Medica . . . .* Venice.

Mendoza Varela, E. 1983. *Regreso a la Expedición Botánica*. Bogotá.

Merrill, E. D. 1954. *The Botany of Cook's Voyages . . . .* Waltham, Massachusetts.

Millican, A. 1891. *Travels and Adventures of an Orchid Hunter*. London.

North, M. 1892. *Recollections of a Happy Life*. London and New York.

Northen, R. T. 1970. *Home Orchid Growing*, third edition. New York.

O'Brian, P. 1987. *Joseph Banks, a Life*. London.

Ovid (Publius Ovidius Naso). *Metamorphoses*.

Pagani, C. 1991. Perfect men and true friends: the orchid in Chinese culture. *American Orchid Society Bulletin*, no. 12.

Paracelsus (P. A. T. Bombast von Hohenheim). 1658. *Opera Omnia Medico-chemico-chirurgica* . . . . Geneva.

Pliny the Elder (Caius Plinius Secundus). *Historia Naturalis*. Venice edition, 1476.

Recchi, N. A. 1651. *Rerum Medicarum Novae Hispaniae Thesaurus . . . ex Francisci Hernandez* . . . . Rome.

Reinikka, M. A. 1972. *A History of the Orchid*. Coral Gables, Florida. Reprinted with emendations in 1995 by Timber Press, Portland, Oregon.

Reveal, J. L. 1992. *Gentle Conquest, the Botanical Discovery of North America* . . . . Washington, D.C.

Rowan, M. E. R. 1898. *A Flower-Hunter in Queensland & New Zealand*. London.

Rumphius (Rumpf or Rumph), G. E. 1741–1755. *Herbarium Amboinense*. Amsterdam.

Sander, F. 1886–1891; second series, 1891–1895. *Reichenbachia, Orchids Illustrated and Described*. Saint Albans, England.

Schulze, M. 1892–1894. *Die Orchidaceen Deutschlands, Deutsch-Oesterreichs und der Schweiz*. Gera-Untermhaus, Germany.

Stewart, J., and W. T. Stearn. 1993. *The Orchid Paintings of Franz Bauer*. London and Timber Press, Portland, Oregon.

Swinson, A. 1970. *Frederick Sander, the Orchid King*. London.

Theophrastus. *Peri Phyton Historias*. Translation into Latin: *Historia Plantarum*. Amsterdam edition, 1644.

Thornton, R. J. 1812. *Temple of Flora* . . . . London.

Tournefort, J. Pitton de. 1694. *Elemens de Botanique* . . . . Paris.

Tournefort, J. Pitton de. 1717. *Relation d'un Voyage du Levant* . . . . Paris.

Tragus (Bock), H. 1546. *Kreüter Buch*. Strasbourg.

Turner, W. 1568. *The Firste and Seconde Partes of the Herbal* . . . . Cologne.

van Rheede tot Draakestein, H. A. 1678–1703. *Hortus Indicus Malabaricus* . . . . Amsterdam.

von Hagen, V. W. 1949. *South America Called Them, Explorations of the Great Naturalists*. New York and London.

Warner, R. 1862–1891. *Select Orchidaceous Plants*. London.

Warner, R., and B. S. Williams. 1882–1897. *The Orchid Album* . . . . London.

Whittle, T. 1970. *The Plant Hunters*. London.

Williams, B. S. 1894. *The Orchid Grower's Manual*, seventh edition. London.

Withner, C. L. 1959. *The Orchids, a Scientific Survey*. New York.

Sources of Illustrations

Illustrations for the indicated pages were kindly provided from the following collections.

Lindley Library, Royal Horticultural Society, London
13–15, 20, 22, 24, 29 below, 30, 43, 45, 48 below, 49, 51, 52 below, 53–56, 59 above, 62 above, 65, 67 left, 68 below, 71–75, 76 above, 78, 79, 80 below, 81–85, 90, 101, 102, 103 left, 105, 118–128, 132–152, Plates 1–16, jacket

Biblioteca del Dipartimento di Biologia Vegetale, Università degli Studi di Roma "La Sapienza"
19 below, 23, 31, 33 below, 42, 44, 46, 47, 48 above, 52 above, 57, 59 below, 64, 76 below, 80 above, 110, 116, 117, 155, 157–171

Biblioteca dell'Accademia Nazionale dei Lincei e Corsiniana, Rome
16, 17 above, 18, 19 above, 32, 33 above, 34, 36 above, 37–41, 89, 92, 95, 103 right, 104, 106–109, 112, 129, 156

Servizio di Documentazione dell'Istituto Nazionale per la Grafica, Rome
17 below, 35, 36 below

Royal Ontario Museum, Toronto, photograph by C. Pagani
94

Sotheby's, New York
87, 97 below

Accademia Carrara di Belle Arti, Bergamo
97 above

Index of Orchids